Michael Riley

ONLY HUMAN

Michael Riley (signature)

ASBURY PARK
PRESS

HOME NEWS
TRIBUNE

266

For my wife, Susan,
and the boys: Josh, Chris, Alex and Sam

Acknowledgments

You never know where the angels are hiding, but over time, you get to recognize them along the pilgrim road.

I've been blessed to meet more than a few of them, these messengers of the Most High, and most of them would rather die than hear themselves referred to in such sacred language.

But that's just tough for them.

The best angels are inveterate gamblers, taking risks and rolling the dice, and I need to thank them:

The Rev. Christopher Drew, who first suggested that an irreverent 16-year-old might someday make a good minister.

Richard Aregood, who took a look at my first rambling attempts at writing and introduced me to people who might be interested: Thanks for your friendship and sage advice about life (some of which I've actually taken).

Dick Hughes, editor of the Home News Tribune, who was responsible for calling whatever it is I do, "Only Human," and later, luring me away from pastoral ministry to the fleshpots of professional journalism.

My colleagues at the Home News Tribune were extraordinarily generous with their time when I arrived in their midst in 1997 with absolutely no experience as a journalist.

My new friends at the Asbury Park Press are not quite as generous, figuring that, by now, I ought to have some inkling of the nature of the job. But they do pretend to find the daily minutiae of my personal life endlessly fascinating, for which I am extremely grateful. To Ronna Sutow, my editor, for her tireless efforts in attempting to persuade me that the cheap laugh isn't always the best laugh.

Thanks as well go to Evelyn McConnell, Bob William and Gary Schoening for their work in making this book an object in the real world, instead of just an idea in my head.

I want to thank my friend and co-worker Bill Zapcic, who took chaos in the form of scattered computer files and brought order, by filing 10 years worth of "Only Human" by subject and date, and did it with grace and patience and wit.

And finally, I want to thank the old high-rolling seraph himself, Bob Collins, publisher of the Asbury Park Press, for "getting it."

Copyright© 2001   •   ISBN: 1-891395-74-2

Contents

Growing Up

Marriage

Life

Kids

Funerals & Weddings

Pop Culture & Church Life

Big Adventures

Foreword

People often ask me how I, a man presumbly called and touched by God to minister to his gentle flock, found myself hip-deep in what is widely considered to be the Sodom and Gomorrah of American secular humanism: journalism. Note: These are not generally the same people who ask how an obvious heathen wound up as a Baptist preacher in the first place.

But in either case, the answer is the same – it was an accident and God's hand was in it.

The fact is that I became a newspaper columnist because a book I picked up in a used bookstore in Boston told me it was easy: "All you need to do is look at your local newspaper and see what you can write about that they don't cover, and tell them you can do it. You may not get paid, but you'll see your name in the paper."

All of which turned out to be true, at least in the case of The Medford Mercury, the local paper in the small Massachusetts town where I pastored a small congregation. In time, a friend of mine gave some of my columns to her father, who gave them to a big-shot Philadelphia newspaper guy, who told me that Dick Hughes at The Home News might be interested.

He wasn't – at least as long as I lived in Massachusetts.

A year later, in 1990, I moved back to New Jersey – one more of those "accidents" with God's fingerprints all over it. Dick Hughes remembered me, and "Only Human" was born. Seven years later, timed to coincide with my midlife crisis, he offered me a full-time job at the paper.

Depending on your world view, I'm either lucky or blessed.

I tend to think it's both.

We are storytelling animals, and I get to make my living now telling tales – out of school, out of my life, out of my ever-patient wife and sons, out of my hardscrabble faith.

As unique as each of our stories is – your stories and mine – they are, I believe, the same: We're all headed home.

What follows are some of the sights I've seen along the way.

Michael Riley

Michael Riley
South Amboy, N.J.
April 2001

From the Editor

Mike Riley is a reporter and columnist for the Asbury Park Press. He is also an ordained minister. Some pastoral duties are not unlike what a journalist does: comforting the afflicted while afflicting the comfortable; finding the humanity in the events of the day. Mike writes about life, in all its glories and disappointments. He has a writing style that is easily understood, yet underlying that is a strong intellectual understanding of religion and how it plays out in people's lives.

Most religion writers and columnists write about religion as a theological essay. Mike takes theology and spirituality and applies them to everyday situations. That allows people, whether they agree or disagree with Mike's point of view, to gain insight into the human condition and how it relates to a higher power.

Mike began writing columns for a small newspaper in Medford, Mass., in 1985 while he was pastor of a church in the area. In 1990 he moved to New Jersey and Dick Hughes, editor of The Home News (now the Home News Tribune), had the foresight to begin publishing Mike's columns. Mike chose to become a full-time journalist and moved to the Press in 1998. The Home News Tribune continues to carry Mike's columns, and he remains the newspaper's most popular and recognizable byline.

Mike has always written from the perspective of his own personal experiences: stories drawn from his family, his friends, his church. And while people may read some of his columns as being irreverent, they are about life – and life is not always reverent. But Mike always finds a way in his columns to get back to a spiritual context.

Mike is a remarkably gifted storyteller. His pieces are filled with clever word choices and turns of phrases in the best Irish tradition. His good humor and good nature are evident in his work. But he is also a thoughtful, concerned person who is very serious about his responsibilities as a man in society, a father, a friend, a journalist and a theologian.

The phrase "Only Human" is, in Mike Riley's mind, an epithet that ultimately ends in blessing and hope.

Ray Ollwerther
Executive Editor, Asbury Park Press

Growing Up

Surviving a taste of God's elixir

I DRANK STOLEN WHISKEY AT THE AGE OF 10 and drank freely offered mother's milk for the first time when I was a grown man. In between, I've tasted snails and squid and a lover's tears. I've eaten crow, choked on my own rancid words and downed huge slices of gooey humble pie.

But the liquor and the milk connect me in some odd way to that odd part of the Bible when John tasted God's word on his tongue and in his gut.

My parents were not drinkers. Closest thing I've seen to teetotalers this side of Mormonism. Once in a while, Dad would break down and have a beer when Uncle Paul got pushy about it.

But he'd only have one.

Mom and Dad didn't have many friends, at least not the sort of friends who would know if they were regular elbow-benders. Friendship took a kind of effort my parents just didn't have to give. Getting through every hard-luck day without the sky falling in on them or the ground opening up and swallowing them whole seemed to take all their time and energy. No time for friends, and booze would only slow you down when it came time to sift through the rubble and start over again.

Dad came home from work one morning laughing. One of the guys at the plant had given him a Christmas present. That was funny enough, but the real hoot was that the present was a bottle of Scotch. He set the tall, striped box with the bow on top on the kitchen table so that Mom and I could get a good look.

"That Al is a piece of work," he said, shaking his head and chuckling.

Then Dad put the box in the cabinet under the sink next to the steel wool and floor wax.

And there it sat. Untouched. Untippled. Month after month. Until one day they left me alone for a few hours.

Four fingers of hooch in a Flintstone jelly glass. And oh, how it burned on the way down, but oh, how warm it felt in the belly. I drank just enough to make my head swim. I washed the jelly glass and poured water in the bottle so it was always full.

The real joy came in the getting away with something. Mom and Dad never found out. I remember when Dad took the bottle out of the cabinet, saw how pale the liquid was and told me you could always tell when whiskey went bad. He poured it down the sink.

I never developed a taste for hard liquor, but I always try to get away with stuff.

A dozen years later, I watched Sue feed our son with God's own mammary manna. Sometimes, she used a vacuum thing to pump her milk into baby bottles. Sue called it "expressing milk." "Express milk" always conjured up images of cows strung out on methamphetamine: "Mooo, man! I'm hurtin' real bad."

There it was, thin and blue and rumored sweet, the stuff of life for my infant boy. How could I not taste it, share this experience with my first born? Four fingers in a Flintstone jelly glass. I gagged on the first taste.

A snootful of the Devil's brew and one sip of God's sweet elixir: Seems about par for the course for us sinners.

In the book of Revelation, the last book of the New Testament, God has an angel feed a little scroll to John. John tells us that it "was sweet as honey" in his mouth, but it curdled his gut (Rev. 10:10).

God's word can make you sick to your stomach as surely as rotgut and mother's milk. And for about the same reasons. God's word is filled with the words of men: ugly, vicious words, sinners' words, drunk on power and pain. But the Lord's sweet words of love and grace will not nourish us unless you receive them with the trust of a newborn child.

At the right moment, though, four fingers of God's word, straight up, can knock you silly and send you heaven-bound.

"Nobody believed my dad"

WHEN I WAS 16 YEARS OLD, my father was arrested for stealing four spark plugs from a Kmart in Mantua. Nobody believed his story that it was all an accident, a misunderstanding; that he meant to pay for the spark plugs; that he had stuck them in his pants pockets for safekeeping, afraid they would fall out of the bottom of the shopping cart, and forgot they were there when he left the store to start the car so it would be warm when his wife finished going through the check-out line.

Nobody believed him.

Not the "snot-nosed, smart-assed punk kid" of a security guard who touched his elbow outside on the sidewalk next to the mechanical horsy ride and said, "Can you come with me, sir?" Not the cops at the police station who made out the complaint against my father, who might have had sympathy for him, but had seen it all too often to listen to him.

I believed him, because that's what sons do. We believe our fathers, believe in them, even if (and maybe especially if) they are not bound to us by blood, but only by love and fate.

The only father I ever had, the only dad I ever knew, was, in fact, my grandmother's second husband. Charles Riley was pushing 40 when he took me into his home and his heart after I was dropped on his doorstep eight years into his second marriage. I don't think he had much of a chance to be a father before me, even though he had a son from his first marriage, a marriage that more or less ended around the time my dad came home from work and found his wife with her head in the oven. (She lived, but the gas certainly took the bloom off that particular rose.)

My dad never mentioned his other son, his namesake, and never sought him out. And the only evidence the boy ever existed was a faded black and white photograph dad kept hidden in the back of his sock drawer, along with his discharge papers and a deck of naked-lady playing cards.

We never escape the past with all its wars and lusts and regrets. It just hides in the dark and haunts us all our days. My dad died more than 20 years ago, and I cry sometimes because as hard as I try, I cannot remember the sound of his voice. But I am as sure as I am of anything in this world that my father tried to swipe those spark plugs.

I believe that, for once in his life, my dad wanted to get away with something. He was a man without the brains or the guts to get away with anything, proving, I suppose, that brains and guts may be overrated. And God knows, whenever he tried to stand up to life, life would smack him around some and tell him to sit the hell back down.

I sat in the courtroom when they called my father's name. When the judge asked him how he pleaded, he said, "It's been taken care of, your honor."

My dad had been led to believe a friend of the family had pulled some strings, and he would be let go. It was obvious the judge and the prosecutor had no idea what he was talking about.

But the judge looked down at this sad and frightened little man with the downcast eyes, the shame-burdened shoulders, and pitied him.

"Go home, Mr. Riley," the judge said.

My father drove us home, home to the trailer park next to the truck stop on Route 295, home to the one place he might feel a little bit loved, a little bit strong, and where the rough justice of this world might give way to a little bit of God's mercy.

Something to give thanks for?

I COME FROM A LONG LINE OF UNGRATEFUL WRETCHES, so Thanksgiving was always a rather awkward time for me when I was growing up.

It's not like the Rileys didn't receive what could be termed blessings; it's just that they seemed to be strictly hit-or-miss affairs so fragile, so fleeting, so damned hard to hold on to.

By the time any of us got around to clearing our throats in an effort to offer up a prayer of thanksgiving, the blessing was usually gone. It had vanished into the dust and dirt kicked up by the hard work of getting through every grinding day. Gratitude seemed to us a luxury, one more thing we couldn't afford.

But every year in late November, we'd give it a shot. Some Thanksgivings, my mom, dad and I would make the long drive to my dad's sister's house in time for dinner.

Aunt Kate and her brood were the only people on either side of the family who would have anything to do with us, so you might think we were thankful for their invitation. But then, you didn't know Aunt Kate and her clan. Aunt Kate was a nice-enough person: a short, stout, long-suffering woman. I imagine her suffering began not long after she married her husband, a man known to me as Pappy.

Pappy built the house they lived in with his own two hands. But Pappy liked his beer, which explains why the whole structure tilted a little, the floors listed, the walls whistled in a strong wind and there were steps in odd places for no apparent reason. Kate and Pappy had two children, adults by the time I was 10.

Their son, Spike, lived with them all through my childhood. A few years before I was born, he shot himself in the head when he found out his wife was cheating on him. The bullet didn't kill him, but it left him blind and more than half-deaf. His sister, Sissy, went through husbands and lovers at such a rapid clip that her son and daughter were never quite sure whom to call Daddy.

Sissy's son, Michael J., was a hulking brute of a boy, who, although three months younger than I, took great joy in thumping me soundly every time we met. Michael J.'s little sister was a harmless, chubby brat. A snarling, yippy, three-legged dog rounded out the picture.

These were my kin, the group my mom, dad and I chose to celebrate Thanksgiving with. A family portrait painted by Norman Rockwell on a particularly bad acid trip, this group of misfits and cretins had made friends with failure all their lives. If Tennessee Williams had met this crowd, he would have sobered up right quick.

Not that there weren't good times. Pappy was always slipping us kids the dregs from his bottles of Shlitz; we'd sneak up and steal Spike's cane, which was always good for a laugh when he had to go to the bathroom and couldn't find it.

By suppertime, thick blue clouds of cigarette smoke hung in the kitchen, yellow light glinted off the brown beer bottles, and people who never thought about praying suddenly thought about praying.

"Who the hell is going to say the goddamned grace?" Pappy would yell over the blaring TV.

I always did, a lot of pressure for a kid. But I was the smart one and the only one who'd ever been to Sunday school.

"Dear God," I'd pray. "Thank you for this food. And this family. Amen."

Those prayers taught me something. Namely, that a merciful God would not smite me for lying through my teeth. At last, something to be thankful for.

Can a man forgive a boy's cruelty?

"Deliver me, I pray thee, from the hand of
my brother, from the hand of Esau . . ."
– Genisis 32:11

FROM THE SEVENTH GRADE TO MY LAST YEAR OF HIGH SCHOOL, Richard and I were best friends. If we had been just a little bit younger when met, we would have sealed our covenant with a rusty penknife, dirty forefingers and our clean, red blood.

As it was, Richard and I shared more than blood. We shared what only two boys on their way to becoming men can share. We shared the questions that we couldn't bring ourselves to ask anyone else, questions about girls, mainly, about what they looked like, really looked like, what they felt like, what did they want, and how could we get some of whatever it was that they wanted.

We shared adventures playing in the rusted-out buses and burned-out trucks that sat scattered like Stonehenge behind the truck stop next to the trailer park where we lived.

When we grew too old for those games, we played at other games; sneaking cigarettes under the overpass, crawling through a hole in the fence so that we could see as well as hear the almost-dressed women on the big screen at the Parkway Drive-In, trying to convince barroom bouncers that, appearances aside, we were 18.

Mostly we shared our dreams. Richard wanted to fly. He wanted to be a Marine like his father had been. He wanted to fly the jets his father had never flown, and in a dream I alone heard, Richard wanted to fly out among the planets, among the stars, leaving behind his failures, his sad father and his alcoholic mother.

My dreams were more gravity ridden. I wanted to go to college and find out what college girls felt like. Even after I saw the light at 16, I just wanted to know what nice college girls felt like. Richard and I shared our dreams night after night, year after year, in a back booth at Jack's Diner. Jack's was a truckers' diner, and we'd watch the truckers flirt with the waitresses and the waitresses flirt back.

One time we watched Dan Rather or somebody come to Jack's Diner to interview striking truckers. We watched Dan Rather's or somebody's eyes widen when the truckers slammed shotguns down on the countertop and said things like, "By God, no truck's gonna ride past here."

Mostly it was quiet at Jack's except for Richard and me when we'd argue, which we did a lot, and for which we were once banished from the diner, the waitresses claiming that we had reactivated some lady's St. Vitus' Dance. Our exile was extended when we suggested that the food might have something to do with the lady's ague.

Night after night, we'd play the jukebox, talking over the truckers' songs and the rockers's songs. We'd watch the headlight scream into Route 295 and Richard would watch the stars. We nursed our Cokes, hoarded our french fries, and never left a tip. We wanted time both to keep us there and move us along. And when the check came, Richard always paid.

Richard always paid in a lot of ways. He and I were at the bottom of our group of trailer park peers. There is not much lower anyone can go than onto the "B" list of the social register of a mobile home park. I had that certain something that passes for a kind of Oscar Wildean wit. It was not nearly as worthwhile a skill as making rude noises with one's armpit, but it saved me from being the lowest of the low – that was Richard. Average, dull Richard. My friend Richard.

He was tried and convicted every day in that place. He was pilloried and savaged, drawn and quartered, and set up and knocked down in the hundreds of ways that only teen-agers can come up with to put their lesser in their place. A little slower, a little thicker, a little more awkward than the rest, Richard paid relentlessly for bad genes, for the sins of his group.

And me? Like Saul of Tarsus, I approved. Unlike Saul, I joined in the ritual stoning of Richard. He'd look up at me when his face was in the dirt and later, when his face was put in far worse places as the attacks became words that broke not flesh but spirit, not bone but soul. He'd seek me out of the crowd that hated him, that had to hate him, that lived only to hate him.

His eyes would shame me with their hot tears, their anger and their knowledge of betrayal. "How could you?" the eyes asked. "Why?" they'd call out.

It would end, the scapegoating, and Richard and I would go to Jack's Diner, never to speak of the betrayal. I wasn't much, but I was all Richard had. He'd sold his birthright for a mess of pottage. And I'd stolen something of value from him, although at the time neither of us could even guess at the price.

We grew up and away, as friends sometime do. Richard joined the Marines, but never flew. He got busted for smoking marijuana in the barracks. He left the Marines and works now at a dead-end job with no family and few friends. I gave him that.

I taught Richard that you have to watch your back all the time. You let your guard down for a second, and even your best friend, your brother, will turn on you. Richard taught me, too. He taught me what I am and who Jacob and Esau were, and a little bit of the way Jesus was.

I stand now, in the night, across the river, and I wait in fear for my friend to come. Jacob the heel. Jacob the grabber waits for Esau, Jacob got from his brother a gift of grace and love that he did not deserve. I wait in the darkness next to the river and wonder if a man can forgive a boy a dozen years down the line. I wrestle not with angels, but with the past, in the night, hard by the black river.

Weak man did best he could

IF MY FATHER HAD BEEN A MEEK MAN, he might have inherited the earth. It didn't work out that way.

If you had seen my father, you might have figured him for a meek man: the way he stared at his steel-toed work shoes and never looked you in the eye when you talked to him, the way he shuffled when he walked away, his head still down. That's not meek. When Jesus blessed the meek, he was talking to brave souls who, by a deliberate act of will, turn away from pride and anger to practice gentleness and mercy. The meek are strong.

My father was not a strong man. Nor was he brave. More or less a coward, he spent his days ducking for cover.

And I was so ashamed of him for a long, long, time.

I remember once, when I was 12, we skipped out on the rent and moved in the dead of night to get away from all the black people in our neighborhood. Black people scared him. They outnumbered him, he thought. They always seemed to have nicer things than hard-working white guys like him. Jews scared him, too, although I don't believe he even knew any Jewish people. He'd heard things, though, about how they waited in the shadows. How they ran the world.

Somewhere along the line he'd been poisoned somehow. It ran like acid through him and made him hard and hollow and bitter. It made even his dreams ugly. I think my father wanted to be a truck driver at one time in his life. Maybe it meant freedom for him, a chance to see some things. But later, much later, the only time I heard about that dream was when we were driving in our used car somewhere and somebody cut us off in traffic.

"I wish I had a truck," he'd say. "Nobody'd screw with me then." And then he'd lean on the horn. Like it mattered. Like it made any more of a difference than anything else in his poor, sad life. I know he had another wife somewhere in his past. And a kid. But he never spoke about either one. I saw an picture once of the little boy buried in the back of a sock drawer. The little boy couldn't quite manage a smile.

As far as I can tell, my father showed some guts just one time in his life.

When the daughter of his second wife showed up at his doorstep pregnant and scared, Charles Riley said to his stepdaughter, "We'll take good care of the child. He can stay with us. We'll make him ours."

And he did. He raised me, and adopted me, and tried his best not to poison me with the ignorance and ugliness and fear that ran through his own veins. I don't know where he got the courage. He was 48 years old when I was dumped on him. He had been married to my grandmother for eight years.

As a father, I know how brave you have to be to make your sons safe and strong in this world. I pray for that kind of courage every single day.

My father didn't have a clue about the way this world works. All he knew was that whatever it was you had, somebody was going to try and take it away. He didn't have the grace and mercy of the Lord's love to fall back on or to gain strength from, because he was afraid of God. He was probably more afraid of God than he was of blacks or Jews, if you want to get down to it.

But I believe that God sneaked in the window of all the places we lived and made His home with us. Without being asked, He blessed my father. My father gave me what meager gifts he had, and miracles happened. Like a few crumbs of bread and a couple of tiny fish multiplied by Jesus so long ago, I grew up stronger and braver than the man who took me in. And I know that where heaven is, so is my dad. And he's not afraid anymore.

N'er do well uncle still a human being

THE WORLD WAS MORE OR LESS AT PEACE 15 YEARS AGO when I saw my first dead soldier in a hospital morgue in Camden. Hospital morgues are not easy places to find or to get to. The dead are messy reminders that life is fragile and not forever. There is something slightly distasteful about the dead anywhere, but even more so in hospitals, where getting on with the business of life is the goal. And so hospitals tuck their morgues away from the eyes of the living, in the basement, say, or down some relatively untraveled corridor. It was down just such a hall I went to find and to identify my grandmother's brother, my Uncle Roy.

When I found the morgue, it seemed to me I had been there before, and of course I had been there through all those TV cop shows I'd seen where actors shoot the breeze next to another actor playing dead under their noses. TV had told me just what to expect.

There was the harsh softness of the fluorescent lighting, shining on the stained linoleum and on the rows of chrome doors that hide those with no more secrets to keep. There was the cold. There was the diffident attendant in dirty sneakers and that godawful green hospital tunic to lead me to the right cubicle and to pull the body out of its box as if he were pulling out somebody on rollers working under his car in his driveway.

There was one thing missing from the morgue, though. It didn't smell. There were no odors, not even the chemical clean smell hospitals are famous for. It was as if even odors knew this is no place to linger.

I stood there while the attendant pulled at the sheets so I could see my uncle's face. It took much longer than I had imagined. There was so much linen and so little of my uncle that for a fleeting moment I thought he'd made a break for it when no one was looking, made a break for the sunlight, for the world of beating hearts and cold beers. But no, there he was, just small in death, needing a shave, lost for a second in whiteness.

My Uncle Roy died from too little love and too much booze. I don't know much about him even though he lived with us off and on for years. I think he was married once, although whether it was the marriage or the wife that failed to make it to the time when I knew him is up for grabs. He did have a tattoo with a woman's name in a heart on his arm. Wives come and go, marriages end, but tattoos are pretty much forever.

He was a mechanic when he worked, which was not often, but he kept an expensive set of tools under his bed, "just in case." He was waiting, I suppose, for the call to come in the middle of the night to tell him the president's car had broken down in front of our mobile home. He was ready.

Uncle Roy fought in World War II. My clearest memory of him is hearing him tell his story about what happened one time while he fought the Nazis in France. It was one of those war stories that gets better each time it's told. The details get sharper in the retelling. What was said and who did what grows longer and yet clearer with each recitation. I'm convinced, though, for reasons that are not entirely clear to me even now, that the 100th time the story is told is just as true, if not even more true, than the first.

My uncle's story reminds me now of one of the themes of Studs Terkel's oral history of the Second World War, "The Good War." For many of the men and women who fought in that war, they were never so alive as in those times and those places. Everything since has been but shadow or echo.

Uncle Roy's war story was about how he was in France on a routine patrol with his unit. Suddenly, a shot was fired and he was down and rolling and bleeding in the dirt. He didn't know what happened to the sniper in the tree, although he was sure he saw a women smiling and laughing as she fired down on them.

Uncle Roy was dragged, still bleeding, by his buddies to a place of safety, if not shelter. There was somehow a German POW with his group, and this POW said, in broken English, he could save my uncle's bloody, torn up leg. And he did. There was no anesthetic but somebody had a flask of whiskey, so they used that to clean the wound and to deaden the pain.

The war ended. The fighting was done, the battles past. But Uncle Roy's pain stayed with him, along with the metal plate they later put in his leg. The whiskey stayed with him, too: gallons and gallons of it down the gullet, down the years, warming some cold place in some secret place in him.

I said my uncle lived with us off and on. When his disability check came from the VA, he'd be off for two or three weeks until the money ran out. Then he'd take the bus back to our trailer, coming in smelling like he'd eaten some kind of dangerous candy. There were times when he'd come into my room late at night and I'd have to get up and shoo the snakes off his bed or swat the flies swarming in his closet.

Uncle Roy died in a dirty one-room apartment in Camden that some friends had set up for him for when he came calling flush with Uncle Sam's money. There may not have been snakes or flies there in that flophouse, but there were plenty of cockroaches to keep him company or busy.

He died, someone found him a few days later, and he was taken to the hospital morgue until somebody came forward to say, "I knew him. That's Leroy Dougherty."

They buried Uncle Roy with his Purple Heart.

There aren't really any morals to this story. Well, maybe two or three: Booze is bad for you. War is hell and can claim victims long after the shooting stops. Everybody should have somebody to love them.

What I really want to say, though, is that everybody's story is important to God. And it ought to matter to us. Uncle Roy did not amount to a hill of beans in anybody's eyes, even and maybe especially his own. He was a n'er do well, and not a very good one at that. He was not likable or lovable. But he was here. And if he's somewhere else now, I hope God cleans him up, gets him a shave and gives back to him whatever this world and its war took from him.

A song of life, amid the mollusks

I USED TO WORK IN A CLAM BAR, and not one of those sissified, gentrified, fern-filled clam bars with lots of chrome and track lighting either. I worked in a real clam bar, a filthy, nasty clam bar, a place where customers came to experience that heightened sense of danger that comes from knowing you might be eating tainted shellfish. This was in the '70s, back before bungee jumping made bad clams obsolete. Ambience was not something this clam bar had. Ambience was something you might be driven away in at the end of your meal.

Competition for the job was stiff. Everybody in my neighborhood wanted to work there, gutting white-fish, steaming shrimp, boiling lobsters and shucking clams, notwithstanding the fact that clams are the singularly most disgusting creatures God ever made. A raw clam, sitting on a half shell, looks like something hocked up on the sidewalk by unshaved, baggy-pantsed men who spend their twilight years sharing park benches with pigeons and brown paper bags filled with quart bottles of Thunderbird wine. Come to think of it, most of the customers who sidled up to the counter for a half dozen clams on the half shell looked like men who spent a good deal of their time discussing the relative merits of wines sold in screw top packaging. You would be surprised, though, at how picky folks can be when it comes to the way clams look. People apparently want to slurp down bivalves in pristine condition, and woe betide the clam shucker whose knife happens to mangle the clam. "Look at this!" grown men would say. "You've ruined the clams!"

Leaving aside the very real epistemological question of whether the phrase "You've ruined the clams" makes any sense, clam shucking is a true art form, one I was ready to tackle. But not right away. Even though I had come highly recommended for the job by a friend who worked at the clam bar, the owner decided I should start at the bottom, so to speak, and sent me to another corner of his farflung seafood empire. I spent a summer in a loft in Camden, putting labels on jars of the owner's own brand of horseradish and cocktail sauce, which he sold to local restaurants. I felt it was a small sacrifice to make if, at the end, I might get to wear the proud T-shirt identifying me as an employee of Admiral Spunky's Clam Bar.

The real reason I was not allowed to start working at the clam bar right away was that the owner had heard I was a religious man, and he wasn't sure that a devout believer would fit in at the clam bar. Lord knows what he thought I might do: Lead the customers in saying grace, say last rites for the lobsters, turn the customers' wine into water?

Religious people were, in his word, "shaky," and he wanted to expose me to the rock-solid people he had working for him. People like Bill.

Bill looked like Charles Manson on a bad hair day. Short, sullen and wiry, he didn't shake my hand when we were introduced. Understandable, since he had a machete in one hand and a dirty horseradish root in the other.

The horseradish factory was basically a two-man operation. ("Used to be I did this by myself," Bill was fond of muttering. "Don't know what I need you for." And since he had the machete, I never argued.)

Bill would wash off the horseradish with a hose, hack it up with the machete and throw it into a big silver vat to be mashed up with water and vinegar. Bill would put the finished product into jars, the jars into boxes, and then bang his machete on the ceiling, which would be my cue to climb down the ladder and bring them up to put labels on them.

It was hot, dull, repetitive work, except for three or four times a day. I'd be at my label machine, mindlessly going about my business, and then: "WAAAHOOOOOUUUUP!" Bill would let out this ungodly scream.

It seems that the final ingredient to go into the big vat was a minute quantity of extract of mustard gas. (That's right. The same substance the Geneva Convention outlawed as a weapon of war was pressed into service as a shrimp condiment.) Bill would hold on to a vial of the stuff, and when he let it go, the effect was akin to some poor blighter in the trenches of Verdun getting a taste of the kaiser's gas.

I never got used to Bill's intermittent screaming. My boss always wondered why six or eight labels out of every batch were cockeyed. It was because I jumped every time Bill screamed.

Back before the business expanded, Bill used to make the horseradish in a room in the back of the clam bar. The story went that one evening Bill picked up an old rifle that had been hanging on the walls for a long time. Just fooling around, he sighted the gun and squeezed the trigger.

An ancient bullet went rocketing through the walls of the clam bar and finally bounced off a customer, bruising his leg. The manager gave the shooting victim a free bowl of oyster stew for his trouble, which suited the customer just fine. (You see why this was a great place to work?) Not long after, they moved Bill to his lonely room in Camden.

There was a pattern to Bill's life. He spent his time holding on to dangerous stuff, and when he let it go, all Hell broke loose. Mustard gas, old bullets, what have you. In that, Bill is exactly like all the rest of us.

We all hold on to dangerous stuff, stuff that will kill us, and we hang on to it just long enough to do the most damage to everyone around us. That's what sin is.

Eve held onto the apple long enough to let Adam get a taste of it. Judas held onto 30 pieces of silver long enough to decide he would hang himself.

We hold on to bottles and needles and envy and anger and lazy lies because we don't know if we have the strength to face life without them. We let them go in horrible ways, because we want folks to hurt the way we do.

The sad, funny truth of the matter is that we don't have to, because God is in the business of holding on to dangerous stuff Himself. God holds on to each and every hazardous one of us and promises never to let us go. He gives us "shaky" ones faith, which is the one truly reckless and dangerous thing in this world that we may keep forever.

Bill probably still is screaming somewhere, letting ammo fly. My prayer is that in all his holding and letting go he may feel the touch of a hand that will hold him forever, and that his screaming may become a song for his God and for every one of us holding on to and dying for all the wrong things. A song of life and hope amid the clams and crabs.

Finding God in the bargain basement

YOU GROW UP PRETTY QUICK IN THIS WORLD when the flap of your underwear has been permanently sewn shut. You learn patience, for one thing. And how to throw a good right hook when some other wiseacre 8-year-old mouths off about something he wouldn't even have noticed if he'd been attending to his business in the lavatory and not looking at other boys' unmentionables.

It was no accident that I owned so many clothes sold as "slightly irregular." Mom went out of her way to buy the things. She made special trips to get the stuff. Once a year, she and I would take the train to Philadelphia to get my "good clothes." Down into the basements of big department stores we would go. By the harsh, greenish light of the fluorescent bulbs, she would search out the big tables that held the factory seconds, jostling out of the way women twice her size in order to find a pair of "Husky" corduroy pants in my size.

There were always plenty of fat-boy pants on the slightly irregular table. They had inseams that looked as if they had been sewn in some miserable Third World sweatshop. But these pants were 30 percent off.

"Nobody will know the difference," was Mom's battle cry from underneath the mean streets of Philadelphia. She uttered it as she loaded up on bell-bottom pants made by someone who had never seen a bell (or pants, for that matter), shirts with one sleeve a good three inches longer than the other (and a couple of extra button holes thrown in for good measure), and the aforementioned trick underwear. "There are kids in China who would be grateful to have nice clothes like these, so quit your bellyaching," she would tell me.

Once I got a little older, I pointed out to her that in Mao's China, conformity was prized above all things and anyone caught wearing slightly irregular anything would be hauled off to a re-education camp so fast it would make your head swim. She accused me of being a communist.

We always stuck to the basements of these stores. I heard rumors, of course, that on the floors above us there were goods made by skilled artisans who took pride in a perfectly tailored pair of skivvies, inspected by tough folk with a keen eye for detail. These goods were displayed beneath bright white light, reflected in the crystals of dozens of chandeliers. Those places were for people who threw their money away, people who wouldn't know a bargain if it walked up and bit them on the fanny. Not people like us.

The one saving grace of these trips was when we stopped at the Automat for lunch. The Automat was to me the swankiest place in the world: Hot food that you pulled out of little doors, just like on "Star Trek." People took their time there. It looked like some of the regulars might even live there. Businessmen in thousand-dollar suits sat cheek-by-jowl with guys whose clothes had slipped past slightly irregular into mostly rags.

When I was 10, the Automat was what I imagined the Kingdom of Heaven would be like. Looking back, it seems to me that my slightly irregular underwear and hot meals at the Automat were part of what made me into a Baptist.

Mom and Dad were no help at all when it came to finding an off-the-rack religion to wear. But John the Baptist appealed to me. He was slightly irregular right from the get-go, him with his camel-hair coat, which stank when it got wet, and his Automat locust-and-honey casserole. John preached God's judgment on dandies and losers alike, and the losers at least took him up on his offer of baptism so God could fit them for a custom-made new heart.

God would send someone to straighten out their inseams and even up their sleeves. And Jesus would take us all up the escalator to the great hall of Heaven, filled with light and all the good stuff.

I'm a man now, with gifts to give to God, but I am still my mother's son. I give God what I have that is slightly irregular, namely my three boys: Josh, Chris and Alex. And I hope He's happy with them, because with this merchandise, there are no refunds or exchanges.

Dad's swearing didn't break any commandments

Things my father taught me
Part 1: The deeper meanings of the Third Commandment.

MY DAD WAS A PRODIGIOUS AND PROFLIGATE SWEARER. When he felt the world somehow was turning against him—which, to hear him tell it, was pretty much all the time—he would let loose with a mighty string of profanity. It was his way of letting the universe know he knew what it was up to.

He wasn't happy about the way life always turned out to be uphill and unlucky for him, in defiance of all the laws of probability and physics (which would seem to guarantee that he would, at least once in a while, catch a decent break). And he chose not to suffer the dirty tricks of fate in patient silence. He'd always wanted to be a truck driver, but life pretty early on had kicked the stuffing out of that dream, so he settled for cussing like a truck driver.

He had his standards. There were certain words he wouldn't use. Words describing sexual anatomy or practices never passed his lips. He wasn't a big fan of abbreviations. Other folks could get by with SOB or BS, but my dad saw that as a sign of laziness. If the United Nations had ever needed someone to act as an instantaneous translator for ethnic slurs, my old man was their man.

But his favorite swear words were religious words. He would invoke the name of his Savior or call down the wrath of the Almighty at the drop of a hat. I was certain, as a 7-year-old member of a Baptist Sunday school, that while God might not be all that interested in damning the shattered jelly jar at my father's feet, He would certainly consign my dad to some particularly noxious corner of Hell for playing fast and loose with a name some religions wouldn't even allow the devout to utter.

My father has been dead now for half of my life, and my understanding of what it takes to break the Third Commandment has changed a lot. Dad's language was certainly ugly, and certainly irreverent, but not one of his "Oh, for Christ's sakes!" is what God had in mind when he told Moses: "Thou shalt not take the Lord's name in vain."

God was warning folks not to invoke the power in His name for their own greedy ends, the way people do when they say, "God wants you to vote for me," or, "I swear to God I love you. Now will you climb in the back seat?" It would never have occurred to my father to do that. He invoked the name of God after the jelly jar was busted, when all the power in Heaven couldn't put it back together.

My dad called down the name of God on his own lost and powerless soul. I pray the Lord has since straightened him out.

Part 2: How to steal a Christmas tree.

Lysenkoism is the genetic theory that acquired traits can be passed on from generation to generation. It is today a completely discredited scientific theory, but you couldn't prove it by the Riley clan.

My father (actually my grandmother's second husband and not even related to me by blood) was a complete klutz. The internal combustion engine was a complete mystery to him. The construction of a tool shed in the back yard was as difficult for him as the Great Pyramids (and took about as long to complete). And I am as mechanically disinclined as my dad.

I would help him now and then with some project. Jesus said something about the blind leading the blind, but I never got that far in Sunday school, so I never realized the trouble we were in. My father would sweat and swear and get mad at himself and me for our incompetence.

"Do I have to draw you a diagram?" he would yell. It took me until I was 30 to realize that, yes, he probably should have. It would have saved us both a world of aggravation. Today, when my kids ask me for help with a project, I say, "You'll have to draw me a diagram, son."

One year, when I was 9, we bought a new artificial Christmas tree (we never had a live Christmas tree – why get a new living thing every year when an ugly aluminum one would last a few years and not catch fire, to boot?), and when we tried to set it up on Christmas Eve night, it proved to have all the wrong parts. It would not make a tree. So at 10 o'clock, my mom, dad and I drove to a supermarket parking lot to steal a tree.

My dad was climbing over a chain link fence when the cops caught him. I remember staring out the back window, watching my father in the police headlights, head down, jangling the change in his pockets, trying to explain the whole sorry mess. The policeman eventually helped my dad put the cast-off tree in our trunk.

On the night when God gave the world a break in the coming of His Son, the world finally cut my dad a little slack. Sometimes, this world is a good place to live.

Some prayers are "close enough"

Things my father taught me, Part 3: How to pray.

MY PARENTS STEERED CLEAR OF BANKS AND HOSPITALS. Just didn't trust 'em. Banks, because, well, with F.D.R. dead and gone, there is just no telling what sort of perfidy those bankers are into. To this day, my mom believes compound interest is some sort of shell game designed to fleece the rubes. She keeps her money in envelopes marked FOOD and RENT.

As bad as banks were, hospitals were worse. They took you to the cleaners, and then they killed you. My father never got tired of telling about the time he went to the hospital soon after he left the Army. Something had gone screwy with the circulation in his legs and he was sent to the hospital, where his legs promptly got worse. They turned black and there was talk of amputation.

One night he woke up and, forgetting the doctor's instructions that he not get out of bed, he walked to the bathroom. And was healed. His trip to the john (which, with each retelling, took on the dimensions of a dip in the grotto at Lourdes) had shaken something loose in his legs, leaving the doctors dumbfounded and with no choice but to let him go.

My father figured as long as he ignored whatever doctors told him to do, he'd make out OK. My mother was a little more sophisticated. She conducted years of research (mainly by watching every episode of "General Hospital" from 1965 on) and came to the conclusion that doctors could be brave and decent folks. But she also knew that hospitals primarily were places where they could carry on their sordid little adulterous trysts. A patient could have his heart monitor playing the one-note flatline rumba for days before anybody found him.

Mom had one other piece of medical information tucked away her in her noggin. I have no idea where she picked it up, because I swear I never heard one of the doctors on "General Hospital" mention it. Mom was convinced that every illness known to man could be cured with a high-colonic, or "physic," as she referred to the procedure.

"What you need is a good physic," she'd say whenever I'd start to look a little peaked.

"I'm fine, Ma," I'd reply. "It's only a scraped knee. Just toss me a leech, and I'll be OK."

Thus was the health of the Riley family preserved for years.

And then my mother's brain went on the fritz. I had just turned 15 when she had the stroke. One night she came home from a friend's house staggering and incoherent and was rushed to the hospital in an ambulance. She didn't want to go. That much she knew, even with her synapses misfiring all over the place.

I stayed behind so I could tell my Dad when he got home from work at about 1 a.m. From the time I told him until the time she returned home three weeks later, he was a lost soul.

Mom was in a coma for a week, and my Dad would sit by her bedside and cry.

Once, early in her stay, a doctor told him he'd have to sign a release so they could do a test on her. When my Dad asked what kind of test, the doctor made a terrible mistake. He told my father. "We're going to put some radioactive dye in her so we can take some pictures of her brain," the doctor explained.

All my father knew about radioactivity was that it was somehow connected to the big bomb that made Japan lose the Big One. Hospitals frightened him, doctors intimidated him, and here he was being asked to sign on to some horrible nuclear experiment with his wife.

He looked at the form for minutes while it trembled in his hands. The doctor kept looking at his watch.

"Sign it, Dad," I ordered him.

He looked at me with the eyes of a child. "What?" he said, coming up from some dark place.

"Just sign it. Everything will be all right."

He scribbled his name and handed the release to the doctor. At that moment, I hated my father. Hated him for being stupid and weak. Hated him for not taking care of us. Hated him until the next night, when I heard him pray.

I was in my room, and he was sitting in the dark, at the kitchen table and talking to my mother as if she were sitting next to him.

"You have to get better, honey. You have to. I can't make it without you. Please come home."

Over and over again.

And even though, at 15, I had no faith in God and my father never asked God to do anything for my mother while he talked and cried, I knew that what my father was doing was praying.

God knew it, too.

There are groanings that, in the words of Scripture, are "too deep for words." He was speaking to his wife, but that was as close as he could get to the Lord in that sad time.

It was close enough. My Mom recovered fully, with my father's prayer and without a high-colonic in sight.

Rewards of faith outweigh the risks

Things my father taught me, Part 4: The recklessness of faith.

MY FATHER APPROACHED THE PROSPECT OF RETIREMENT the way a man in a dream will approach the rim of a black and bottomless pit: he's just there, suddenly, high up in the mountains with no clear understanding of how he got there or how to get home, and the darkness beneath him seems to whisper again and again, "Jump! Jump!"

Which is to say, he was not looking forward to it.

My old man thought retirement killed people. He would come home from work in the morning, put his lunch pail down and announce, "Jerry Feeney died. Seven months. Seven lousy months." Which mom and I took to mean that Mr. Feeney had departed this veil of tears just seven months after he left the employ of the Westinghouse Corp.

The burgeoning mortality rate of recent retirees was a subject of morbid fascination for Dad, especially as he eased up on his 65th birthday. "They're dropping like flies," he would say to Mom.

It wasn't only these actuarial hijinks that scared my father. When he was 63, he suffered a major heart attack, which he always saw as sort of Death's Welcome Wagon: "Hi, Mr. Riley. It's me, Death. I was in the neighborhood, thought I'd drop by and introduce myself. Can I call you Charles? Listen, Charlie, I can't stay long now, but I'll be back before you know it. You take care of yourself. Oh, by the way, Jerry Feeney said to say hello."

His second heart attack, a year later, was such a small thing, nothing more than a myocardial glitch, really, that Dad was sure it was only Bad Luck come calling, not the Big D himself. But that second heart attack got Dad to thinking he should come up with a plan of action to fool Death into thinking he was still busy even after he retired.

Which is how we got sucked into what became known as the Great Hobby Frenzy of '75.

My father never actually liked to do anything, so any hobby he picked would have been his first. His only criteria were that it be cheap and that it done at home—while sitting down.

So one Saturday morning, we drove to a toy store where my parents picked up a dozen plastic models: race cars, rockets, battleships and the like. That night, my parents invited me to join them in a night o' fun building stuff.

I passed. This was a train wreck I saw coming from a long way off. My father had never been good at sticking Tab A into Slot B, even when it came to assembling something as large as a lawn mower. With a half-scale model, Tab A is nearly invisible, and Slot B has been covered over with glue, the narcotic properties of which had caused it to be outlawed in 12 states. Thirty minutes into it, Dad was pounding the chassis of a classic ambulance into pieces with the flat of his hand, cursing up a storm, the little red siren light for the top of the ambulance stuck to his glue-encrusted forefinger.

Firmly convinced that hobbies would kill him faster than retirement, Dad began to see himself as a doomed man.

Until, with mere weeks to go before he punched out his time card for the last time, the landlord of the trailer park where we lived, a man by the name of Mr. Fabrizio, offered my Dad the chance to manage a motel he owned in Ocala, Florida: "Go down and try it out for a couple of weeks. Think it over."

Dad said he'd take the job. No need to think it over. My parents put our trailer up for sale and we moved to Ocala. For 10 days.

Dad knew nothing about motel management. He had been a storeroom attendant all of his adult life. They taught him how to do it in the Army. He was stationed in the Aleutians during World War II, as far from any field of battle as any human being could be.

He went to work for Westinghouse after the war. It was an easy gig. He was a union man. My Mom told me even his bosses didn't mind when he took naps on the job. I couldn't have been more proud.

But keeping books, hiring and firing chambermaids and routine maintenance were way out of Dad's league.

We crawled back to New Jersey with our tails between our legs. But my dad had taken a shot: He went to Florida with the recklessness of a heathen suddenly confronted by the Risen Lord.

Faith is a risky business. You never know what's going to happen next when you give your life to God. Maybe my father should have stuck it out. He died from a heart attack four months after he turned 65.

In the Sermon on the Mount, Jesus asks: "If a son asks for bread from any father among you, will he give him a stone? Or if he asks for a fish, will he give him a snake?" (Luke 11:11)

My dad gave me plenty of rocks and snakes. He didn't always mean to; things just sort of worked out that way. But it is the grace of God in my life that has turned my Dad's rocks into bread, and his snakes into fish. I thank God and my father for them.

May the Father of us all rest my Dad's sweet soul.

Marriage

Weathering the storm of marriage

SOMETIMES, MARRIAGE IS LIKE THIS. I'm out on the prairies of North Dakota, say, or the Texas plains; anywhere big and barren and flat. I'm staring off into the distance, staring at the place where the great bowl of the blue sky meets the razor-sharp edge of the world. There's danger out there, and while I'm safe now, I will not be safe for long. The thunderheads are piling up, miles high it seems to me, and they are headed my way. This storm will be awful and terrible and beautiful: The wind will howl a monster's howl, the rain will sting like acid, hailstones will riddle the Earth like rifle fire. Crops will be damaged; so will hearts and faith.

I see all this before it happens, know it as well as I know the sweet and secret names I call my children. And I know this, too: There is no way to escape this storm, nowhere to go, nothing to be done, except pray, hold on and hope.

Though I am not alone, sometimes it seems that way. Soulmates under one roof may lose one another in the vast tundra of a split-level home. The distance across the kitchen table can be a thousand miles of dry riverbed.

But when these clouds burst, my love will be beside me. Together we will smell the ozone of the lightning-burnt air, shiver in bone-soaked skin and shout ourselves hoarse trying to be understood as the roaring wind carries our words away. We know, my love and I, that these harsh and riven times are no acts of God. Husbands and wives are lightning rods, calling down the thunder upon themselves. Husbands and wives pull up buckets of muddy and brackish water from the dark wells within them and bid the other to drink deeply.

The last storm that Sue and I went through, though, was a surprise to me. It was my own fault: I'd ignored the widely scattered funk in the sky, hadn't seen the bluebirds flying off for higher ground. By the time the whitecaps started breaking against the living room coffee table, it was too late for sandbags, too late for hearts and flowers, too late for anything but slogging through the steadily rising waters.

Like I say, it was my fault. And, hey, it's not just me saying it. Sue could tell you it was my fault. She told me often enough during those tempest-tossed few days: I was away too much, and even when I was home, I was far away, wrapped up in work and self to the detriment of hearth and kin.

In the past, I might have raged against the elements, like Lear on the heath, or Ahab on the Pequod. But both those guys were nuts, and both wound up dead. You can lose your marbles and catch your death when the monsoon hits if you're not lucky or smart. I happen to be both, so even taken unawares, survival instincts kicked in, which meant, by and large, that I kept my mouth shut.

I thought some about how little it takes to make those we love happy and how, so often, we seem unable or unwilling to give even that. I prayed some. And I waited. Two days in, Sue began to launch again into what I had come to call "the litany of wrongdoing." She stopped suddenly, in mid-lit, as it were, and smiled.

"And you know," she said with a small laugh, "you can't do anything right."

The rain ended. Sunlight bent and angled through the water in the air. A bow in the sky appeared, a sign of covenant and memory and mercy. Sometimes, marriage is like this.

Everyday events can be revelations

THERE ARE MOMENTS, EPIPHANIES IF YOU WANT TO GET FANCY ABOUT IT, when you realize your life is seriously out of whack.

You might think one such moment came when Sue and I found ourselves arguing over who would drive Joshua to the emergency room after he was hit by a car on his way to school one Thursday morning not long ago.

You'd be wrong.

Sue and I were both dug in, each believing we were too busy to do it.

"I've got 14 3-year-olds to teach," Sue said.

"Oh, yeah, nobody else can oversee the finger painting," I said. "I, on the hand, am indispensable. I've got deadlines, sweetie, important interviews to conduct as a member of the Fourth Estate. I'm writing the first draft of history."

The conversation went downhill from there.

I don't want to leave you with the impression that Joshua was lying in a bloody heap by the side of the road while this was going on. He was fine, more or less. His foot had been run over by a midsize car. No big deal. It's not like the foot is a vital organ or anything. Heck, it isn't even one of those semi-vital organs like the spleen.

Apparently, 14 3-year-olds trump the First Amendment because I wound up driving Joshua to the emergency ward. And there wasn't an epiphany in sight when I left him and his smelly tire-treaded sneaker there, either. I told him he'd be all right until his mom got there, and I sped to the office. I was 10 minutes late for a telephone interview I'd scheduled. I called the woman and apologized for my tardiness, explaining about the car and the kid and the non-vital foot.

"I don't want to talk to you now," she said. "You need to be with your son in the emergency room. Nothing is more important than that. We'll talk tomorrow.'"

Sometimes, your best epiphanies come from complete strangers. In this case, bells rang out, angels sang. "Of course," I thought. "My son is more important than my job." "Sweet Jesus," I prayed, "What was I thinking?" Jesus declined comment.

I drove back to the hospital and met up with Josh and Sue. It turns out that my son has some kind of genetic anomaly that allows his foot to withstand 3,000 pounds of rubber and steel with no damage whatsoever. The doctors didn't even need to take X-rays.

The three of us went to breakfast in the hospital cafeteria. And there, amid the breaking of bread and the eating of rubbery eggs, another kind of healing took place.

Sue and I each admitted that maybe we'd gone a little crazy.

"Of course," she said, "if we're going to dump a kid in the hospital like some orphaned waif, Joshua's the one to dump. He'd wrap the nurses around his little finger."

She was right, of course. There's no way we'd leave our 14-year-old son Christopher alone for a minute in a hospital. He'd go in for a hangnail and wind up committed to a psych ward.

The boy's a little odd. "So what's the deal with those bowel resections you doctors are always foisting off on the unsuspecting dupes you refer to as patients?" he'd ask after the attending resident asked him how he was feeling.

Call me the prodigal father.

"I have sinned against God and thee," I tell my first-born. "I let the blindness in this world touch my own eyes, and I allowed the illusory demands of this life to lead me away from my true home and my true name. Forgive me."

"Uh, sure, Dad. Listen, can we get me back to school soon? I've got band practice in a couple of hours."

I kissed his forehead and knew again what the grace and pardon of God feels like.

The underwear spoke the truth

LAST WEDNESDAY EVENING, in the underwear aisle of a local Kmart, I received a vision from the Lord.

It was an unsettling vision, revealing as it did the dark, weak hearts of so many men. Of course, God's the expert when it comes to disturbing images. It's the devil who gussies things up, makes them look shiny and pretty to bamboozle the yokels. It was Satan, after all, who showed Jesus, all alone in the desert, all the bright and glistening kingdoms of the world, and told him they were his for the asking.

God, on the other hand, shows a prophet like Amos a sun-spoiled, maggot-ridden basket of summer fruit and says, "The jig is up. You people are way past ripe."

Truth to tell, the whole rotten peaches picture wasn't really germane to what God wanted to show me, which is why he waited until I had a package of "Star Wars" briefs in my left hand and a package of glow-in-the-dark "A Bug's Life" undies in my right.

I hasten to add here that the underwear wasn't for me. I'm strictly a "Batman" sort of guy. These were for my son, Sam, who, nearly 3, had just that weekend graduated from his mother's potty training boot camp. Frankly, I don't understand how Susan has potty-trained each of our four sons in their time in less than 24 hours. When it comes to some things, I'd rather remain blissfully ignorant.

All I do know is that the process involves copious amounts of M & M's and a book called "Toilet Training in Less Than A Day." Sue guards the tome like it contains ancient secrets known only to a handful of practitioners of certain dark arts. I suspect that electrodes might be involved, but I can't be sure because my job has always been to get the other kids out of the house for the day.

You can't argue with success, though. And to celebrate the bum's rush, as it were, of mastering the art of the flush toilet, the Rileys always make a big deal of buying what we refer to as "big boy pants."

So, it was off to Kmart. Decisions, decisions. Is it Darth Maul with a light saber or the glow-in-the-dark ant?

Christopher, 14, was a big help.

"Sam, I've heard that glow-in-the-dark underwear can make you sterile," he whispered in his brother's ear.

Now Sam knows nothing about reproduction. He had his own reasons for eschewing the luminous briefs. If you wear glow-in-the-dark underwear to bed, he patiently explained to us, the monsters in the closet know right where you are, and who needs that kind of trouble?

It was at that moment that God appeared to me in a vision.

"Behold," he said to me, "I show you the beginning of the Midlife Crisis."

I understood instantly what the Lord was trying to reveal.

There are some guys out there – not me, of course, for I am strong and pure – who hit 40 or so and begin to think that they ought not be spending a perfectly fine Wednesday evening standing in a Kmart. Jesus, they pray, shouldn't I be running with the bulls in Pamplona or finding my way up Kilamanjaro and down the Amazon?

"I wish I had nickel a for every doofus who left his wife and kids to go climb a mountain and sip Chardonnay on the Left Bank," God said, "only to wind up with frostbite and a hangover."

At its grace-filled best, life is full of surprises and complications anyway, He reminded me. And love is always a mystery, the way it may come strangely and inconveniently, and even in the sad way it sometimes dies after many years.

You will wind up in some strange places in this world, even without a crisis, saith the underwear. The least you can do is be honest and brave during the journey.

Weathering temporary amnesia of the spirit

HERE'S A TIP FOR ALL YOU GUYS OUT THERE who may be wondering if your marriage is hitting a rough patch. If your wife calls you at work and says to you, "Bring home a quart of milk and a copy of 'Women Who Love Too Much,'" you might as well put your seat in a locked and upright position and buckle up — you're headed into some pretty heavy turbulence.

By the way, if you're the type of husband who would respond to your wife's request by saying something like, "What the hell are you doing reading books?" I can't help you. The only brave thing to do is to get the book and hope for the best.

I'm not saying there's no danger involved. It's risky business, a bombed-out landscape, a mess of ruins. You may not make it out unscathed. But, for God's sake, sometimes you just have to mount up, ride into the noise, heat and fire of battle. You have to be a man.

Being a man, of course, puts you at a distinct disadvantage. Because a book like "Women Who Love Too Much" isn't just about women with a love addiction. It's primarily about the louts and losers, the oafs and brutes they don't have the temerity to dump. A lot of us guys, apparently, are horrible swamp-dwelling bottom-feeders.

So, for the week or so it took for Sue to wade through the text, I'd come home from work feeling like I was a grunt on point, stepping lightly with a mine sweeper in my trembling hands. I kept my eye on that book, watching day by day as the bookmark crept its way along the pages, and I'd tentatively ask how the book was coming.

Well, as it turned out, Sue is not the sort of woman who loves too much. At least she doesn't love me too much. What a relief. It also seems as if I'm not a bottom-feeding sort of guy, which, you know, is always good to hear.

"That book is good for women who feel trapped in abusive relationships," Sue said. "Not for us."

Which could have been the end of it. But no. Just because I'm not a bottom-feeder doesn't make me a paragon of virtue. Sue's reading another book now, the gist of which seems to be how wives are supposed to handle their husband's constant complaining about the burned pancakes at breakfast.

In point of fact, in 20 years of life together, I have only complained about 1 1/2 meals. There was the purple chicken incident, where Sue poured a few gallons of cheap red wine in the pot with a chicken in attempt to make coq au vin. And then there was the ground beef and egg concoction that looked so awful I left the table.

"You know, it's not like you've never burned the pancakes," I said to Sue. "I always figured that the only thing that would come from it would be syrup dumped in my lap and then I'd have to make my own pancakes. 'Shut up about the damn pancakes, already,' would be my advice to husbands."

"It's not the pancakes that are the problem," Sue answered. "It's deeper than the pancakes. It's what the pancakes represent."

"But I like your pancakes," I said.

"That's not the point," she said, a slight edge creeping into her voice. In all seriousness, I knew what the point is. (It was either get the point or find myself awash in self-help books.)

You get married and there comes a point where " 'til death do us part" seems like an awful long time. Because we forget, sometimes, we men and women, what true love is, and passion, and hope.

It's an amnesia of the spirit, an Alzheimer's of the soul. A husband or wife becomes an emotional stranger in the house, in the bed. Our minds wander, and our eyes, and even our hearts, sometimes. If you can remember, you can weather the stormy sky and bring the plane home safely.

The search for the blue-light wedding present

SUE AND I HAD PROBLEMS.

In the first place, the bride to be was not registered at Kmart, which meant that what could have been a nice, simple task – picking up a combination ax sharpener/cappuccino machine or some such, going through the express lane and getting home before dark – turned into a shopping trip. A shopping trip for someone else.

I hate shopping trips. A shopping trip makes me feel like one of those dowser guys looking for underground water by walking around with two sticks crossed in front of themselves, jerked hither and yon by mysterious water-seeking forces. Except that I walk around with my wife in front of me, jerked hither and yon by mysterious bargain-seeking forces.

Bouncing around from sweat socks to kids' sneakers, from oven mitts to curtain rods – boing! boing! boing! – until Sue finds the one bargain that will give our little lives meaning. And that's when we know what we're looking for.

This wedding present business, well, we were up the gift-giving creek without a moderately priced paddle. Our task was made difficult by the fact that this couple had been together a while. They had a house and a houseful of the stuff that makes a house a home. To further complicate matters, we hadn't been to their home since they had remodeled the place, so we had no idea whether a chartreuse bath mat would be appreciated.

I never buy gifts that presume to define the giftee's idea of taste because, after all, one man's delicately carved, hand-painted, ready to grace any coffee table flounder sculpture is another man's delicately carved, hand-painted, hide it in the bottom of the closet until the idiots who gave it to us come for dinner monstrosity. (Sue would say that I eschew taste in gift-giving because I don't have any, but that's another story.)

There is nothing like having to buy a present for friends to show you how little you know about your friends. But we persevered, Susan and I, in our quest for the Holy Grail.

If the truth be told, after a couple of hours of wandering in a land once known for an ugly display of naked consumerism called the flashing blue light special, neither of us much cared if the Grail was holy or not. We would have settled for any old grail. A slightly irregular grail would have been just fine. We would have jumped at the chance to get a marked-down floor model grail.

In the end, it came down to one of two presents. Susan found something called a picture collage. This was a large picture frame with several spaces into which you could put smaller photographs. Nice. Pedestrian.

I, on the other hand, found the helium. A small propane tank of helium and a bag full of balloons, packaged in brightly colored cardboard can be had for less than you might think. It's a perfect wedding present.

The possibilities are endless. You can blow up the balloons. You can suck a little helium and talk in a high squeaky voice. Well, OK, the possibilities aren't endless. But even after you run out of helium, you still have an empty tank, which can serve as a nifty doorstop.

We met up in the sporting goods department. Sue showed me her picture frame. I showed her my box 'o' fun. Susan said she had nothing against helium. Helium was a fine element, right up there at the top of her list of favorite elements. But if I thought for one minute we were going to give our friends a load of gas for a wedding present, I was about four protons shy of a molecule.

We went with the picture frame. Such are the compromises that keep a Christ-centered marriage together.

(An informal poll of eight of our closest friends later—none of whom knew the wedding couple—went seven to one against me. Only my pal Martin, who has the Ph.D. in behavioral neuroscience, said he would have gone with the helium. But Sue said his vote didn't count because anybody who makes a living sticking needles into the cocaine-laden brains of laboratory rats, in the belief that such endeavors would lead to a cure for cancer, obviously is even more protons short of a molecule than I am. She had a point.)

Gift-giving is a holy affair. I thought about that as I sat in a church last Saturday and watched my two wounded friends stand at the altar. Wounded, like all the rest of us, by sin and sin's betrayals, and yet joy shone in their faces.

Life always takes more from us than it gives. That's the way life is. And what it doesn't steal, it breaks, so that the baggage we carry around with us rattles around in our lives, a noisy and jagged reminder of all our wrong choices and failed loves.

And yet, on a cold Saturday in February, two people gave themselves the gift of the other. One way to look at it is to say that, given who they are and where they've been, neither one is getting a bargain. That's the way the devil sees it, and he hopes like Hell they will see it that way as well.

But when a person gives all that he has and all that he is to another, and is received in grace by the heart of the one he loves, miracles happen. My broken friends are made a little bit whole by the vows they make and the rings they share and the gift they give.

And the priest gives them Jesus Christ. In a crust of bread and a sip of wine, they are given all that Christ has to give: His blessing, His strength, His joy, His abundant life. That is what marriage is: The gift of love sealed by Christ. And the Devil can't have it. And the world can't take it.

In the name of Christ, then, Susan and I gave our friends a Kmart picture frame. May the pictures placed there reveal the healing, redemptive joy of two people who, in a fallen world, have found one another and the Lord who makes them one.

Spouse's drool a no-no topic

IT IS HEARTENING TO CONSIDER that even after being married for over a dozen years, you may find you still have things to learn about your wife.

You might learn, for instance, that she does not appreciate having a discussion of her drooling plastered all over the newspaper in front of God and everybody.

I tend to think of these surprises as little gifts from God, given to us to keep love ever fresh. But I could be wrong about that. I've been wrong before.

I don't have to check in with Susan every time I write about her. After 13 years, you and your spouse build up a certain level of trust. But since I am not a completely insensitive lout, I will occasionally run stuff by her before I send it off. Except when I forget.

"I can't believe you would mention my spittle," Sue said after reading last week's column.

"Drool. Not spittle," I replied. "I would never mention your spittle in a public forum. What do you take me for anyway? Besides, I'm sure I talked it over with you."

"Muttering to me while I'm in the shower does not constitute talking things over. And while you did mention open mouth, violently loud snoring, about which I was none too happy, you didn't say one word about spittle."

"Drool, honeybunch, not spittle," I said gently.

Another good thing about being married for a long time is that you keep your reflexes honed dodging small thrown objects.

I may forget some things, but others I will always remember. I remember the night I met Susan.

It was a moonless, spittleless September night in 1978 on my first day back at college. I had left a year before because of financial difficulties and was ready to resume my role as perennial sophomore. It was an evening of renewing old friendships and making new ones.

My usual method of doing this involved being rude and insulting to anybody who happened to walk into the student lounge. In the interest of saving time, I gave everyone an opportunity to take an immediate dislike to me. This is the kind of stuff that passed for charm in the late '70s.

An old girlfriend had told me she might bring her new roommate, a transfer student named Susan, to meet me.

"Sue has been hurt a few times," my old girlfriend explained. "She thinks all men are jerks. You will, I trust, do nothing to disabuse her of that notion."

I was looking forward to this. I screwed up. And so did Cupid.

You know Cupid. Blind guy. Dark glasses. White cane. Sociopath. Goes by the name of Maurice. I don't believe in love at first sight, but if I did, it would have applied to what I felt for Susan. Big green eyes and a smile that would not quit.

During the course of the evening, while I was regaling everyone with wisecracks, a blind transfer student named Maurice took Sue's hand, telling her he needed the tactile sensation to get to know people. And he would not let her hand go. He stroked it and rubbed her arm over and over again. Sue was obviously uncomfortable, but her graciousness and style would not allow her to remove it. All the other guys in the room thought it was a hoot. (I guess most men are jerks.)

I was seated to the side of Sue, and I rescued her. "So, what's your major?" I asked, which allowed her to turn to answer, gently extracting herself from Maurice's grip.

The next day, Sue and I ran into each other. She thanked me for saving her. And I did something I swear I had never done before: I apologized for my rowdy, off-color behavior. Susan looked at me and said, without a trace of condescension, "That's OK. I knew what you were trying to do."

From that moment, I realized I would have to marry this woman. Or kill her. She knew too much. She had seen my wretched insecurity, my desperate need for attention. Love, you see, is not blind. Love sees into the secret heart of things. And goes right on loving. You either have to love back or destroy it.

Which is one reason why Jesus was murdered. And what is marriage but being Christ for someone and allowing that person to be Christ for you "to know and be fully known," as Paul wrote?

Of course, seeing too much is what has gotten me into my current matrimonial pickle, so maybe I had better sign off. When you've been married as long as I have, you learn when to shut up. But you don't learn it fast enough.

Reminiscences of a first Thanksgiving

IT WAS OUR FIRST THANKSGIVING AS HUSBAND AND WIFE; we were six months into this troth-plighting business called marriage.

When you are newly wed, the calliope never stops playing, your hearts never beat except as one and your brain never works. Reality never come anywhere near wherever it is new lovers find themselves. Reality won't even stop over for a cup of coffee until you've been married for 18 months or until the baby gets colic, whichever comes first. Then, of course, Reality moves in pretty much forever. But until then, it's like this: We'll never go to bed angry at each other," we'd say and we'd laugh. "We'll always be sensitive to each others' needs," we'd say and we'd laugh, "We'll always tell each other truth," we'd say and we'd laugh.

Ha Ha.

On this first Thanksgiving of our new lives together, we were going to cast aside tradition. We were going to be bold and innovative; no mundane turkey and fixins for us. Sue was going to cook a genuine gourmet French meal, the *piece de resistance* of which was going to be coq au vin, which is how I came to be asked by the woman I love more than life itself what I thought of the purple chicken on my plate.

Unmistakably purple

I'm not sure how the chicken came to be purple, but it was. It was unmistakably purple. Bright purple. Glow-in-the-dark purple. At the time it happened, I was busy watching Bullwinkle the moose and every high school kid in America with a tuba floating over or marching down Manhattan streets on TV. I have a theory, though.

Park of the meal's charm was to be its authenticity, and its authenticity came in part from the French cookbook Sue used to prepare the meal. It was a real French cookbook, which is to say, it was written in French and it used some more obscure portion of the metric system in its instructions. My guess is that Sue misread some measurements and this poor chicken was dropped into a huge bubbling vat of some recently vintaged wine. (Given our budget at the time, this was probably the same wine chosen by a sizable majority of the paper-sack crowd watching the Macy's parade from New York City alleys through rose-colored eyeballs.)

I can only assume the chicken was left there too long. Way too long. If I were asked to give someone just one piece of advice to help in the journey through this veil of tears, way up near the top of the list of possibilities would be this: Never, ever, at any time, under any circumstances eat a purple bird.

I didn't know diddly about French food, but I knew something was not quite kosher. Nevertheless, with the calliope going, the heart pounding, the brain not working and Reality sunning itself in Barbados, I dug right in. "Frere Jacque!" I said. "C'est la vie!" I said. "Apres moi, le deluge!" I said. I took a bite.

Words fail

I couldn't even wash it down because there was no wine with which to wash it down because the stupid chicken had sucked up every drop of wine in the house. I looked up and saw Susan, sweet Susan, and she asked me, "How is it?"

Now Susan is not a stupid woman. She knew this purple chicken was a dead duck in the edibility department. All she wanted from me was a word of hope, of loving encouragement. What I said was this: "It stinks. Do you think McDonald's is open?"

I shouldn't have said that because for that night, the carnival music stopped and Reality caught the first flight back. It is not as if Susan had wanted me to lie, to tell her it was the best purple chicken I had ever had so she could be sure to serve it again and again down through the years. What she wanted was the truth alone, the truth told in love. I could have hugged her and said, "It's all right. You'll try again. Let's break open a couple of cans of Thanksgiving chili." But I didn't.

The hammer of truth

There are those of us who wield the truth like a sledgehammer or shotgun. We tell the truth the way some fight guerrilla warfare – with a real slash-and burn mentality. We use the truth to strike out, to be cruel. To hurt and to cripple.

Preachers do it, too, in the pulpit and out. "The Truth hurts," we say, "and if you can't stand the stink, then stay away from the Mad Dog, bubbling away in the kitchen."

What we wind up with is a lot less than the truth, because if the truth sometimes hurts, it always heals, and once in a while it does both at once. Healing takes words, but more than words, and so does truth-telling.

"Be ye doers of the truth," it says in John's Gospel. Do the truth. Live life openly and honestly, creatively and lovingly. A parakeet can tell the truth, for God's sake. It takes a person to do it.

Emily Dickinson said, "Tell the truth, but tell it slant," which is one way of doing the truth and probably a good part of the reason why, when somebody asked Jesus a simple question, he told stories about dumb virgins and sly thieves, about crooked judges and profligate brats. The truth gets inside of you as you wrestle with the story and becomes part of you.

"I am the truth," said Jesus. He said this, too. "You shall know the truth and the truth shall set your free." Jesus sets us free from the lies we tell ourselves, free from telling the truth like dropping a bomb. He sets us free to live in Him, in the Truth which is Him.

We are free to do the truth in ways that redeem the broken people among us and the wounded one within us. We are free to give thanks for the music that never ends, and to be thankful that the tears shed for purple chickens are not in bitterness but in sweet sadness that moves us to joy.

Life

For my funeral, three songs of myself

WELL, YOU'LL BE HAPPY TO KNOW I'VE FINALLY PICKED MY FUNERAL SONGS.

This isn't the sort of job you want to leave to your well-intentioned but grief-stricken loved ones after you kick the bucket. God only knows what kind of maudlin ditties they'll come up with for your final send-off. I mean, "In The Garden" is a fine hymn, but darn it, it just doesn't say "Mike Riley," you know?

I've worked hard on this list for years. Not as a full-time job, you understand, but here and there, now and then, when I've had a few minutes to ponder the hard realities of my own mortality. It's been a list in flux: "Amazing Grace" has been off the list and back on a dozen times at least. I finally decided against it because, when it comes to funerals, "Amazing Grace" has been done to death, as it were.

But now, I've got the list. Three songs designed to make my funeral a testimony to the powerful love of God and my own departed sensibilities. These babies are written in stone.

I will admit my joy in finding just the right songs was lessened somewhat by the fact that I didn't have anybody to actually sing them.

The obvious choice would have been Susan, the hypothetical Widow Riley.

She wanted no part of the festivities.

I can't sing at your funeral, she said.

I'd be too distraught, she said.

Too sad, she said.

Yeah, right. Like this is all about her.

She has a point, though. The last thing you want at a funeral is the featured soloist sobbing hysterically. It really casts a pall on the proceedings. What you need is a talented friend who isn't going to be too broken up by your shuffling off this mortal coil.

I've got one of them. She's agreed to sing at my funeral, lo, these many years hence. Well, as long as she hasn't got anything else to do that day, like, say, wash her car or her hair.

But you take what you can get in this world. Especially when you're dead.

I'm sure this friend will do a fine job with the numbers I've selected.

I think we'll open with a hymn. I've always liked "Be Thou My Vision" with its rising otherworldly melody and words like "High King of heaven, my victory won/May I reach heaven's joys, O bright heaven's Sun!" It's catchy, you can dance to it (although the Baptists in attendance would rather be with me in the casket than admit to that) and it's theologically sound. We can make it a sing-along.

Somewhere along about the Lord's prayer, we'll slip in a version of Bob Dylan's "Every Grain of Sand." Written in 1980, back in the day when Dylan and Jesus were best buddies, it's a strange melancholy song, with a kind of self-referential elegiac air about it.

"I am hanging in the balance/of the reality of man/like every sparrow falling/like every grain of sand," Dylan sings. I don't know what the heck he's talking about, but maybe that's the point. Who knows exactly what death brings? We're all riding on the wings of hope when it comes to the Great Beyond.

After the Gospel's been preached and testimonies given about, the wonder that was me ("No, please, stop. You're too, too kind") we'll end with Bruce Springsteen's "Land of Hope and Dreams."

Springsteen's song uses that great gospel/rock 'n' roll metaphor of the train, heard everywhere from Curtis Mayfield's "People Get Ready" to Elvis' "Mystery Train." Saints and sinners, whores and gamblers ride this train, where "dreams will not be thwarted and faith will be rewarded."

It's a song that gives us all a taste and hope of a heaven to come. What more can a funeral Give?

My faith in good deeds is revived

HERE'S MY IDEA OF ROUTINE AUTOMOTIVE CARE.

When you're driving along, and suddenly huge clouds of steam and smoke are rising from under your hood and filling the interior of the car through the heating vents. Simultaneously, you notice in the rear-view mirror that the car is leaving puddles of motor oil in its wake. What look like flames are shooting out the front grill. It's probably time to have your car looked at by a trained mechanic.

My car definitely needs to be looked at.

A couple of weeks ago, I was driving home from work on a Friday afternoon when all of the above happened. I was trying to get to the nearest exit off of Route 18 when, luckily for me, a van pulled up beside me and the driver pointed at my hood.

Like I'm an idiot. Like I didn't realize that my vehicle had suddenly turned into some kind of James Bond deathmobile: "Oh, thank you," I felt like saying. "With all the smoke and steam inside the car, I couldn't see that, indeed, I may be experiencing technical difficulties that require my immediate attention."

Instead, I nodded helplessly and drove onto the exit ramp. The engine quit on me about then, which at least had the advantage of silencing the horrible demonlike noises it had been making. I coasted down the ramp and stopped on the shoulder of the road somewhere in Freehold Township.

Now, some people might look on being lost and stranded as a bad thing. Not me. That damned glass is always half-full as far as I'm concerned.

"Oh great," I said to myself. "I get to have an adventure."

I got out of the car and started to walk down the road.

I didn't get 200 feet before a car pulled up next to me. A man rolled down his window and called out to me.

"Do you need help?" he asked.

I told him about the car and said that I was on my way to find a gas station. He asked me if I had a cell phone.

Once again, I resisted the urge to say something like, "Sure. But you know, it's getting dark, I have no idea where I am, and I figured I could use some exercise."

I just said, "No, sir, I don't."

He told me he'd take me to the nearest gas station (which turned out to be three miles away). We got to the gas station, and they didn't have tow trucks.

The man asked me if I had AAA. I had let it lapse under the apparently mistaken impression that I lead a charmed and blessed life.

"Let me call on my card," he said. He got on the pay phone and gently browbeat the Triple A folks until they agreed to tow the car of his "very good friend, Michael Riley" to his home in Edison. Then he called his home to tell his wife that he would be a little late. He drove me back to the car and we waited for the tow. He stayed with me until I was all hitched up and ready to go.

All I know about the man is that his first name is Milan and that his last name has too many vowels. He seemed to be from India and manages a Taco Bell somewhere on Route 9. He wouldn't take any money. ("You should give the tow truck driver $10, though. They like that," he told me.)

I told him that it is a dangerous business to be helping strangers in the fading sunlight.

"Life is too short," he said to me, "not to help people in need."

I know one more thing about Milan. He's closer to the Kingdom of God than almost anybody I know. He's an angel, a bearer of good tidings.

He makes me look like a piker when it comes to faithful good works. I pass broken-down cars and stranded strangers every day. I've got places to go and things to do.

But not next time. You don't double-cross an angel.

No dead end for these suits, ties

SOMETIMES I WEAR DEAD MEN'S CLOTHES.

But not their shoes: For some reason, the shoes of the dead always seem to crowd my toes and pinch my heels. I wear their suits and ties, though, their jackets and pants. And, for the most part, I've always been grateful for the generosity of the dead.

One could make the case, I suppose, that altruism has nothing to do with it. Once you've been decked out in your favorite or finest duds and lowered into the earth or incinerated out of it, after all, questions of wardrobe are pretty much rendered moot. You really can't take it with you, which is why, as someone once said, you never see any hearses with luggage racks.

Besides which, the dead don't care. Being dead seems to me a full-time job. There's all that decomposing to do, all that waiting for the resurrection. It's enough to keep a corpse busy around the clock. What the dead have to give, they give to gravity and to the soil.

It is the living who bag and box the stuff and offer it to me. They have good hearts, full of hope and sadness, those widows who have, over the years, given me the clothing of their loved ones. But generosity may not be their only motive. Nature abhors a vacuum. Shell-shocked and grief-shaken, those who mourn need to do something, anything, to fill the lonely days. Emptying out a dead husband's closet may be a painful undertaking, so to speak, full of memories brought to life by the sight of a certain coat, the feel of a particular silk tie and the faint traces of their smell embedded in a suit. But it beats going to bed and listening for ghosts in the night.

Maybe there are no such things as ghosts. Yet, what the dead leave behind can have a strange, strong power over us. The most mundane items can bring them back to us. I remember the first time I entered my father's bedroom after his death. I was 18. It was a mid-September morning. I remember sunlight and motes in the air. I remember looking around and saying to myself, "Oh, these were his slippers." "There's his hairbrush." It was if I'd never seen them before. It was as if I'd never really seen my father before. And maybe I hadn't. More's the pity. When I finally cried for him, six months later, I saw his smiling face. But I also saw those slippers and that brush.

A dead man's clothes can surprise me. I'll put on a sports coat, stick my hand in a pocket and pull out a slip of paper; a receipt for a set of spark plugs, say, or a matchbook with some illegible name scrawled inside it. I usually put it back in my pocket. It takes me a long time to throw away these long-forgotten effluvia. Somehow they are my connection to some other life, and I hang on to them as if it were my sacred obligation to do so. Perhaps, I figure, it's one small way for me to honor the dead.

Dead men's clothes are rarely a perfect fit. But then, what is in this world? Our marriages, our friendships, our jobs, even our faith in the God who calls us to live with him in some sweet heaven: they're all a little short in the sleeve, a little long in the inseam, a little tight around the shoulders, a little loose around the waist. And, sooner or later, they all begin to look a little worn and threadbare. But with love in our hearts and grace in our lives, we can grow into the hand-me-down gifts of the Almighty.

For guys like Arthur, you need some rules and some compassion

ARTHUR CALLED ME FROM HACKENSACK THE OTHER DAY WITH BAD NEWS. It seems he's only got two months to live. Of course, in the 2-1/2 years I've known Arthur, he's always had only about two months to live. Something fatal is always rumbling around inside of him.

It was in his legs when we first met. They were going to chop his legs off, probably too late to do anything but guarantee his burial in a special "short man's casket."

Arthur still had both his legs nine months later when he came down with AIDS. "What are you gonna do?" he asked me. "You need a transfusion so the doctors can save your legs, and you get loaded up with bum blood."

It's a good thing that AIDS business was just a false alarm. Otherwise he wouldn't have the strength he needs to fight whatever deadly nastiness now is spreading in him.

I confess. I bear some responsibility for Arthur's current shuffle off this mortal coil. Like the sequoia that falls silently in the primeval forest because there is no one to hear it fall, Arthur does not begin to die in a hurry until someone breaks what I have come to call the First Rule for Dealing With Arthur: Never, ever, say to Arthur, "So, how are you doing?"

To Arthur, "how are you doing?" means "how are you dying?" and there is no end to it unless there is some day an end to him. Which seems unlikely.

The Second Rule for Dealing With Arthur is much like the first: Never ask Arthur what he wants from you. Talk about the weather, sports, or (if you have broken the first rule) about the great medical strides being made every day to cure whatever it is that's killing him.

It's not that he ever wants very much, but what he asks for is rarely what he is really after. What Arthur wanted when he first called and asked me to drop by the motel in Edison where he was staying was "spiritual guidance."

He was, he said, a Baptist and had been one for, well, for a long time (or, I suspect, for at least as long as it took to find the number of my church in the phone book). You would think that after all this time we Baptists could come up with some kind of code word or trick question we could use to identify each other. But no: We've got Baptists without portfolio running willy nilly all over the place. And every single one of them winds up with my number.

I thought this "spiritual guidance" line was kind of interesting, so on my way to visit someone in the hospital, I stopped in to see him. What he really wanted was two cans of tuna fish, a quart of milk and a jar of instant coffee. And to complain about his ex-wife, who, even if he didn't have all these lethal parasites running amok within him, was apparently doing a fine job of killing him by "making his nerves bad."

Over the next year, I would hear from Arthur now and then. I'd make sure he had a roof over his head for a night or two, or drive him to a free clinic, or make sure he had a bite to eat. One thing I would not do is pay the ransom on his dry cleaning. Even suckers like me have our limits.

He's a generally likable guy, even if he is a royal pain. Once, Arthur asked me to drive him to Trenton so he could straighten out some bureaucratic foul-up that was holding up his check. When we got to Trenton, Arthur told me that where he really had to go was York, Pa., and could I drive him across the river?

In for a penny, in for a pound, I always say, so I drove him to some human services office in Pennsylvania, where his last check from that state was waiting for him. I thought to myself, this is great. Four years of college, three years of seminary, and I wind up driving a getaway car across state lines for some kind of welfare heist.

Albert didn't bother me much after that. The last time I saw him was when I put him on a train that was supposed to take him to some Home for Mysteriously Dying Veterans in Virginia. Whether he got there or not, I don't know.

Now and again, I would get a call from a deacon or a minister from some church in Maryland or Pennsylvania. They had a lifelong (fill in the denomination of your choice) named Arthur in their office who said I would vouch for him as the kind of guy who could use a warm bed and a couple of cans of tuna fish.

What could I do? By the time they called me, it was already too late to tell them the Rules for Dealing With Arthur. The toll call alone probably cost more than the tuna.

I would tell them that I knew Arthur, that he got around, that they should in no way pay his dry cleaning bill, and they probably weren't getting taken too badly if they got him some milk.

Now, he is in Hackensack, and in the course of 16 seconds, I have broken both of the Rules for Dealing With Arthur.

What Arthur wants, I believe, although I can't really hear him that well because I'm too busy whacking myself on the head with the telephone receiver, are his clothes. He left a bagful of clothes in my garage once. I told him he could come pick them up any time.

He doesn't want those clothes. He's got a steamer trunk of clothes in the Amtrak station in Philadelphia that he wants me to pick up. I told him that a guy with two months to live doesn't need that many clothes. I think he's going to pick up his clothes from my garage.

Once, early in our relationship, I went to Arthur's room. I was tired and impatient when I said, "Look, what can I do for you, Arthur?"

He met my eyes and said in an even, measured tone, "I don't know. What can you do for me?"

Here's what I do for Arthur: I let him tell me lies that both of us know are lies, because I pray that out of those lies may come the truth that will set him free.

I let him die for me over and over again that somehow he may know that he can live forever.

I get him milk and tuna fish because milk and honey is too hard to come by in this hard land.

I'll drive him over the border because even con men need someone to hear them now and again.

I'll buy a bridge or two from him and hope against hope that in some small way I may be Christ for him. Because whether he knows it or not, that is who and what Arthur really wants.

In the dark of night, the Light of the World comes

THERE ARE THINGS THAT GO BUMP IN THE NIGHT: a big toe against the nightstand, a hairy shin on the coffee table, a fat head into the half-open bathroom door. And, oh yeah, the Son of God comes booming back to life in the dark of Easter morn. He goes bump in the night, too.

I remember a night about five years ago. We were living in Medford, Mass. I was trying to breathe life into a dark and dying church. It was frustrating work. I would catch some of their darkness every Sunday morning as I looked out at the handful of folks who'd come to worship. And I'd die a little bit.

They were good people, and I loved them, but there was nothing I could do for them, except keep them warm and comfortable as we waited for the end to come. I wondered a lot about how it was that God had dropped me into such a miserable place.

We had a 90-year-old organist named Arthur who, on more than one occasion, fell asleep during church. Which wouldn't have been so bad except that when Arthur fell asleep, he really fell asleep. His shiny bald head would come to rest on the keyboard, and his forehead would be playing some godawful chord, four or five notes that sounded like God's own Bronx cheer.

The congregation would gasp. You could see it in their sainted eyes: "Oh, no. Dear Lord. Arthur's dead."

Me, I'm a sinner. I was thinking, "This is just great. Arthur's croaked. Why do these things always happen to me?"

I'd walk over to the organ and give Arthur a little nudge just to see if he still was among the living. He'd wake right up and start playing the Doxology, thinking he'd missed a cue and not dreaming that he'd been dreaming.

"He's not dead. He's sleeping," I'd sigh to myself as I walked back to the pulpit in a resigned funk to finish praying or preaching or whatever it was I was doing before Arthur went KA THUDD on the ivory keys.

It was not a good time for me. I mean, here I was, pulling off a miracle of sorts, raising the dead (or, at the very least, the seriously narcoleptic) in the Lord's Own House, and I took no joy at all in it. The darkness had a hold on me.

Then came the night when the power failed all over town, and the darkness filled up our house. No street lights, no night lights. The clouds blocked out the moon and stars. Just Sue and I going bump in the night.

I had a flashlight, which did what flashlights always do when the power fails: absolutely nothing. So I lit a candle, cursed the darkness and made my way to the room my two older boys shared. The sudden darkness and silence had shaken them up. I sat down with the candle in the space between their beds.

On some other night, in some other place I might have told them ghost stories. I had a doozy to tell them, all about a man trapped in a haunted church, a church filled with ghosts who wanted to live or die, but wanted an end to this spectral in-between existence. The ghosts called out to the man, rattled their yellowed old hymnals at him. They cried and remembered how it used to be. And the ghosts would not let the man alone, and they would not let him leave.

But this scary night was not the time for ghost stories, and so I sat crosslegged on the floor with my candle and tried to calm my sons. And something wonderful happened in that room filled with the smell of little kids' sweat and crayons and clay. A light went on in their hearts, and they asked their father some marvelous questions.

Joshua was 5 years old, and the room caught holy fire when he asked, in the high, clear voice of an angel: "Daddy, can we go to Heaven before we die?"

I swore to him that night that we would. We'd climb into that big cardboard box in the back yard and we would sail away, out past the farthest star. We would find Heaven, and we would carry it with us, and we would bring back it back home. Heaven was ours for the asking.

Christopher was only 3. He could not have cared less about Heaven. His concern was to make it through the night. "Dad," he wanted to know, "was Jesus scared when the lights went out?"

The room burned with the light of a thousand suns.

"Oh, my little boy. Jesus was scared when the lights went out on Him. His Daddy didn't come for him, didn't answer his questions. It was dark when he died, and you can bet he was scared. So it's OK for you to be scared a little bit, my sweetheart. You may be scared, but you remember: The lights will come back on."

I was reborn that night.

Sometimes I think the only thing scarier than when the lights go out is when they come back on. Which is why the gospel accounts of Easter morn are so filled with fear. We tend to think of it as something that happens quietly. But it wasn't. You can't hush up a resurrection.

The rocks and stones that Jesus swore would start singing on Palm Sunday start singing this day. The earth quakes. There are angels rolling away tombstones. Brave men swoon, and braver women shudder.

The very first words the Risen Lord speaks are these: "Do not be afraid."

Why shouldn't we be scared? If God can raise the dead, bring the Light of the World back from the darkness, rout all the demons of Hell, what in Heaven's name will he do to us?

"Don't be afraid," Jesus says, his hand raised in blessing, a smile, that smile, on his lips. "I'm here. And I love you."

What does the Son of God do on his first days back in the dark of this world? He turns the lights on, wherever he goes, flipping switches in the soul and bringing life. He travels incognito, puts on a fake nose and catches up with two disciples on the road to Emmaus.

"What's up?" he asks. They don't recognize him, and they tell him how their dreams turned to ashes when they crucified Jesus.

"You don't say?" the Risen Lord says.

The disciples invite the stranger to dinner. When the moment is right, Jesus takes off the disguise, and a light goes on in the apostles' souls as Jesus disappears.

What else?

He fries up a mess of fish on the beach at the Sea of Tiberias so his friends will have something to eat for breakfast. Jesus the Risen Short Order Cook.

He lets Thomas poke and prod him, lets Thomas get his dirty fingernails into the spear wound in his side. A light goes on. "My Lord and my God," says Thomas . . . In short, Jesus lives.

Wonderful and frightening, Jesus lives.

He calms us, feeds us, teaches us, humors us. With whatever it takes. The Light of the World comes to each of us in the dark, and brings us with him back to life.

Jesus lives, and he lives for all of us: sad ghosts and sinning ministers, frightened children and sleeping organists, idiot apostles and Doubting Thomases. And for you and for me.

Jesus lives. Happy Easter.

There isn't always room for Jesus

So THERE I WAS DRIVING THROUGH THE STREETS OF NEW BRUNSWICK with Jesus dying in the back seat. My windows were down and the radio was cranked way up with Roger Daltrey stuttering and swaggering his way through "My Generation." "Hope I die before I get old," Daltrey sang, which, of course, he never did.

Die young, that is. Daltrey's pushing 50 so hard it's about to fall over on him. I wonder what he hopes for these days, now that a young and glorious death has been denied him.

Jesus, though, lover and giver of life, dying young and in a nasty, shameful way in the back of my Ford, had wished for a long life, or at least a longer one than God gave Him. "Let this cup pass from me," He prayed. Let someone else die this death. Let George do it. But George was busy, and even if he had not been otherwise occupied, George couldn't have handled it. Nor could anyone else for that matter.

Jesus was the only man for this particular job. If He didn't do it, the job wouldn't get done. With sadness, then, and a sense of inevitability, Jesus climbed onto the cross and into my car. He would die before He got old and He would die for old Roger Daltrey and for you and me.

I don't know if Christ appreciated the irony of the situation the way I did. I certainly didn't ask Him. He wasn't up for conversation. He probably wasn't even listening to the music. I suspect He was past hearing.

Past seeing

Christ was certainly past seeing. I had put him as gently as possible in my car. He was lying on His side in the back seat with His head turned so He could only catch flashes of sky and street as we drove up Route 27, but His eyes were fixed on somewhere far away. He was looking hard for heaven, looking for it even when His eyes were shut against the pain.

He couldn't see what I saw as we crawled through traffic: the bodegas and the video stores with garish posters in the windows, posters of powerful men with guns in their hands and blood in their eyes, the world exploding behind them. Jesus couldn't see the bars, two or three on every block, which in a very few hours would be filled with smoke and loud music and young drunks who would spill out into the streets looking for trouble and probably finding it.

The Son of God, who has beheld the glory of the Father and has seen with perfect clarity the dark heart of every sinner, was, for these few moments, blind to the dirty business going on right under His holy nose. In back alleys, bread was being turned into stone, a five-dollar bill became a bag of crack cocaine, a soul went up in smoke just for the chance to be taken to a place where, for just a little while, life wouldn't hurt.

A few blocks over is a woman who, like Lot's wife, only can look backwards. She is turning tricks and, if not turning into a pillar of salt, then into something equally hard and bitter. She gives herself away for pennies, sells her birthright for a mess of pottage. She opens herself in tiny rooms and in the back seats of cars much like my own for men who hunger for God only knows what. The men leave, hungry still, and the woman will look away. She looks back because when she has looked ahead, she has seen nothing. It is not that she doesn't know what to hope for—she has forgotten how to hope.

I know Carl is somewhere on these streets as well. He lives on these streets, begging for small change. "Father Mike," he'll call to me when I walk on George Street now and again.

He knows my name because he's been to my house. I caught him once peeking into my garage. "Father Mike, can you give me one of those bikes?" He's a sad and sick young man.

When he finds me on the streets of his town, I give him a buck or two for cigarettes or blow or Thunderbird. I can't give him what he needs. He wouldn't take it from me anyway. So I give him what he wants. Because it is, Christ knows, a hard world out there.

Look what it did to Him, after all. Left Him hung out to dry, left Him for dead, left Him in the back of an old Ford, left Him deaf and dumb to the cries of His people.

The hookers and addicts, the losers and the deranged, they were His folks, the ones who took to Him, who listened to Him, who were changed the most by Him. We're driving right through His old stomping grounds. Driving slowly, because I'm not in any hurry, and Jesus isn't going anywhere.

Stopping at a red light, I see the great hospital on our left. We're a little late for that. There's no hospital anywhere that could save Jesus at this point. He's just too far gone. And Jesus, who never went anywhere without healing at least one poor leprous schmoe, is in no condition to be healing anybody.

By the time I got Jesus to my house in Edison, He was as stiff as a board. In fact, He was a board of sorts, because the dead Jesus in my car was a wooden sculpture by a Ghanan artist named Michael Gayampo that I had borrowed from the Visual Arts League, an "art for the people" outfit in New Brunswick. I thought I would display it in my church for a couple of weeks.

Before I could do that, though, I had to get Christ into my house, and before I could do that, I needed to get Him out of my car. Which turned out to be twice as hard as getting Him into my car.

An awkward thing

I wrestled with the four-foot, solid something or other crucifix. A cross is an awkward thing. You can't get a decent handhold. I finally got it out and hauled it up my front steps. I was sweating and my fingers hurt. I know the Bible tells me to carry my cross, but where does it say I have to carry my cross and His cross and Him, too?

I first put Jesus down on my bed, but I couldn't keep Him there—there was no room in the inn for Him even now—so I stuck Him in the closet for a few hours before I lugged Him over to church.

There was no place for Him in church either, no place to put Him where He wouldn't be in the way or out of place. He is now on display underneath the coat rack in the narthex.

It is probably true that a lot of our churches and a lot of our homes have no room for Jesus, dead or alive, on the cross or off. And Jesus isn't about to come off this one. Cross and Savior were carved together; they are one and the same, as they should be sometimes.

We settle for someone less than Jesus most of the time, fooling ourselves into believing that the Christ we've got is somehow the real McCoy. We're afraid that if we let the real Jesus into our hearts and homes and churches, there wouldn't be any room left for us.

The real Jesus is big and hard to hold. He's dying all over the place, making a mess. And rising so unexpectedly that He's sure to frighten the hell right out of us. He's always in your face, demanding that you love every crackhead and whore in the whole world. Who needs that kind of grief?

Well, we do. And until we let that big scary Jesus into our churches and our souls, there is no room to become the saints He's trying to turn us into.

Unexpected pearls from mouth of child

SOME SAINTS BLEED.

Suddenly and spontaneously, it is said, the palms of their hands begin to bleed, the soles of their feet darken and moisten and, in the rarest of cases, their sides open up a spear's breadth and a thin trickle of the trunk's sticky red sap stains the skin and heads south. Hours or days later, the bleeding will stop, until Good Friday comes again to the saint, without regard to the day of the week or season of the year.

This is a miracle with a special name. The bearing of Christ's wounds in the skin and bones of a holy person is known as stigmata, and it is an awful and painful expression of God's awful and mighty love for all of us. What the world did to His Son, God now does to some of his saints, and, in this way, holiness becomes not a matter for spirit or soul or will, but for cells and marrow and clotting.

It is, as my mother would say, "just what they get for being holy."

If there is a stigmata of the holy, well, the rest of us bleed and bear scars, too, in a sort of stigmata of the stupid. Not two weeks ago, I had one of my periodic bouts with it, as I traveled my own Via Dolorosa, known locally as the New Jersey Turnpike.

A happy band of pilgrims traveled with me, five of us in all, and all of us headed home as the stars began to shimmer in the hot New Jersey Saturday night. We had spent the afternoon with my in-laws in South Jersey and could not spend the night, so we headed north.

My wife drove so I could read in what was left of the day's light read and do my other job, which is to turn around periodically and yell at my three boys in the back seat.

Somewhere between Exit 8 and Exit 8A, Sue said to me, as before her Larry had said to Moe, and Lou had said to Bud, and Stanley to Ollie: "We'll have to get gas soon." "Oh," said I, with the nonchalance of the straight man. It comes easy to me. What is a minister, after all, but God's own straight man? God's got all these great jokes about grace and salvation, and ministers fiddle around with deadpan seriousness until God gets the punch line out.

"Do we have enough gas to get off the Turnpike?" I asked, because while Jesus warned his listeners about highway robbers on the road from Jerusalem to Jericho, I know about highway robbery on the road between Jackson and Jamesburg — "service areas" where candy bars cost as much as filet mignon and a gallon of regular unleaded is not to be had for less than the black market price for a pound of plutonium.

"I believe we do," said my wife, faith, of course, being the evidence of things not seen.

Love, the Apostle reminds us, believes all things, and I believed my wife's belief. In that moment, anything could have happened and I would have believed. The heavens could have split open revealing the heavenly host, the third horseman of the apocalypse might have hitched a ride on a moving van, Christ himself may have come again to judge the quick and the dead.

What happened was that the car bucked once, twice, and rolled to a dead stop.

The truth may set us all free, but a lying gas gauge and a gullible spouse will pretty much screw you up every time. We were stuck on what surely must be, good intentions aside, the wide road to hell. We were, as in Jesus' parable, five foolish virgins (two of whom, at least, should have known better), with no oil in our lamps, no gas in our car, no flares, no gas can.

And so it was that I set out to help my family. I did this without even asking Sue to do what we normally do when one of us has to do something that neither of us wants to do: go two out of three rounds of rock, paper, scissors. Christian feminism has made great strides but not, apparently, in the realm of walking down the Turnpike in the pitch black night.

I was dressed in knee-length short pants and a black T-shirt. I opened the car door, stood up and tumbled down the embankment into a bunch of briars. Aren't highway workers or chain gangs supposed to take care of these things?

My bloody calves got me back up onto the scary road, but not before I stepped into a muck hole, which covered one leg in a brownish green slime.

I limped about a mile down the road, getting help from a toll worker who called the little van that helps fools like us. You try to maintain a little dignity in cases like these, bloody and muddy and goofy-looking. But you can't. Besides which, these guys have seen it all before. Losers like me apparently are a dime a dozen, crawling out of the darkness on the Turnpike.

One thing the other losers didn't have, though, were prayers on my behalf. My middle son, the 7-year-old who has a real future ahead of him as either a minister or a disgruntled postal worker, prayed aloud for me in the back seat while I was stumbling about, seeking octane and cheating death.

His prayer went like this: "Dear God, thanks for getting us to Grandmom's safely. Help Dad to get help so we can get home safely. Amen."

How many of us in the foxholes and muckholes of this world remember to begin our prayers with a thank you? Not me, for sure.

My prayers that night were pretty much variations on the theme of "O God, don't let the big fast cars kill me." Not a thank you passed my lips. It was all muttering about muck and blood and gaslessness.

Christopher knew, though, the secret Paul let us in on when he was a lot older and had a lot more to worry about than becoming grillwork on a speeding semi. "Give thanks in all things," he writes, and "always."

My son already is bearing in himself the marks of the God who made him and saves him. Blood of my blood, he teaches me the deepest mysteries of our faith.

He prays, too, that God will help his Mom and Dad remember to get gas before we hike our sorry pilgrim selves down the road. It's a silly prayer, childish, ridiculous really. And given who his parents are, absolutely essential.

Kids

We were just doing our duty

FRANKLY, I THINK CHRISTIE TODD WHITMAN, the governor of the great state of New Jersey, bears much of the responsibility for the current situation here at the Riley household. "Too much snow," she said. "State of emergency," she declared. "For God's sake, don't leave your homes," she implored.

So, we did our civic duty, my wife and I, during the blizzard of '96: We stayed put. Which is how Sue came to be unexpectedly pregnant with what will be our fourth child. Personally, I think some sort of Good Citizenship Award is in order here.

Not that Gov. Whitman is wholly responsible for my impending paternity. There is a certain manufacturer of male birth control devices whose quality control department is a little slipshod. According to the box they came in, each item is supposed to be "electronically tested." Who knew that meant two skinny high school dropouts wearing Black Sabbath T-shirts holding each prophylactic up to a 40-watt light bulb? A fuse blows in a basement somewhere, and I'm looking down the long barrel of fatherhood again.

It's exactly this sort of thing that's going to keep America from becoming competitive in the new global economy.

Sue's announcement that she was going to take a little drive to pick up a home pregnancy test was the first inkling I had that we were skinny-dipping in the gene pool again. As she left, the wind slammed the door behind her. Thinking his mom had slammed the door in anger, my middle son, Christopher, 11, asked where she was going. When I told him, he said: "Did you just tell her that she might be pregnant?" That boy and I have to have a talk soon.

Susan came home and retired to the laboratory, where she did whatever it is a woman has to do to find out if her ovum has had "a gentleman caller," so to speak. (Sue begged me to keep this column in good taste. I told her that whatever I write is always in good taste. "Well, better than that, then," she said.)

I waited outside until I was summoned. Call me Igor.

"Michael, could you come here a minute, please?" my soulmate said. I was in the bathroom like a shot. Sue handed me this plastic thingamabob.

"If you can see a pink stripe in the circle, it means I'm pregnant," she explained.

Suddenly, I was back in junior high chemistry class, squeezing lemons onto litmus paper. I didn't see a pink stripe. What I saw was a bright red stripe, flashing like a neon sign outside a strip club: "LIVE! NUDE! ZYGOTE!"

"Maybe it's a false positive result," I offered. Sue gave me the pamphlet that came with the kit: " . . . and don't go thinking the results might be wrong, Bozo! We're 95 percent accurate."

So there we were, face to face once again with the "miracle of pregnancy," and I couldn't help but think, "Been there. Done that."

Sue and I will be 38 when this kid comes out; our oldest son will be 14. We'll be 40 and changing diapers. This was not in the plan. And I don't think it was necessarily in God's plan either. Occasionally, it's true, God will fiddle around with human fertility, so that someone like Sarah can give birth at 90, but I think there are a lot of babies who the Lord would just as soon not have been born: Jeffrey Dahmer, say, or those who die hungry before their first birthday.

Having a child is a human choice. And yet, how can the promise of new life not be good news? Sue and I hung onto each other for dear life. God bless us, we pray, and God help us. We're going to be parents again!

The howl of dogs in the yard

WE ARE NOT RESPONSIBLE FOR EVERY THOUGHT that comes unbidden into our noggins. Some thoughts are wandering junkyard dogs: ugly, mean and better left alone. We come upon them suddenly in the moonlit scrap heaps of our minds – their yellow eyes all aglow, their white teeth bared, a low growl from deep inside their throats. We stand before them, transfixed, rooted to the ground, when we know we should slowly back away. But we stay, begin to consider the unthinkable, and in an instant the dogs are on us and we are lost.

In the hours after Sue and I found out that she was pregnant with what will become our fourth child, I was numb, some odd mixture of joy and dread working its way into my gut, the way I imagine a junkie feels in the moment before the needle hits the vein.

And then it came to me.

We don't have to do this. We don't have to have this child. We could end it soon, end it quick, be done with it before it has a thumb to suck and a heart to break. Nobody would know, and those who found out would understand. God himself knows that this pregnancy is a fluke, an accident that wouldn't have happened if things had worked the way they were supposed to. Who would blame us, Sue and I, if, at the age of 38, we decide that our three beautiful sons are children enough?

There comes a secret thrill with the thinking of dangerous, shameful thoughts, a mirror-image kind of pleasure at knowing you have opened certain forbidden doors.

"I am capable of this," you think. "I am the kind of person who can kill if I need to, who can kill if I want to. Let nothing stand in my way."

It's the sweet pulp of the fruit plucked from the Tree of the Knowledge of Good and Evil. It is the sound of the rock in Cain's hand crushing Abel's skull. It is the howl of the junkyard dog.

How do you give voice to the worst that is in you before it consumes you? To whom can you go when you suspect that even the Lord is filled with disgust at the secrets in your heart?

For me, there is this woman I love. She is sweet and fierce and full of hope. I have loved her for nearly half my life, loved her hard. Susan has seen what's twisted and stunted in me and loved it back to life. We've made babies and raised sons and built something out of the blessings of God. She sat in a chair, as shellshocked as I.

I stood above her and could not look her in the eye. "I've been thinking," I said. "We don't have to do this."

"Yes," she whispered. "Yes, we do." No judgment in her voice, only tenderness. Christ beside her, Christ around her, Christ in her. "We're good at this."

It's simple, really. We, and I speak here only for me and my beloved, have to make a choice for life. We have to make our stand with the living. It's what God has made us good at.

But it ain't gonna be easy. I can kiss my dream of having cable installed by the turn of the century good bye. Guess how much a pastor of a small Baptist church makes? Go ahead. take a guess. What are you, nuts? Take another guess. Lower. Lower. Now lop off another 10 percent and you're in the ballpark (way up in the cheap seats, true, but in the ball park).

I gave my sons a real "gonna be some major changes around here" speech: belt tightening, room sharing, hard work. Alex said he was too old to be the baby anymore. Christopher said he wouldn't mind taking the new baby for walks because "chicks dig that." (It's amazing what a couple of weeks at Frank Sinatra's Camp for Young Swingers will do.) Josh guessed he'd better get a job to help out.

Laughter and trust in God are all any of us have, not to keep the wolf from the door, but to send the yellow dogs of the junkyard scurrying into the night.

"It's time," says the mother

Part 1 - Sam says "Hi!": Notes from the new father of the most beautiful baby in the world.

I. IN WHICH I AM UNDER THE MISTAKEN NOTION I have solved one of the mysteries of the ages - and in which I am roundly disabused of such foolishness by one wiser than myself.

At 6 a.m. Sept. 16 — what is now known around our house as "The Morning of the False Alarm" — my wife, Sue, woke me up to say she's had gas pains for the past few hours.

There is no more avid proponent of the tenet, "Married couples should freely share their feelings," than me; nevertheless, I am a firm believer in the context of such sharing. Six in the morning is just too early to discuss gastrointestinal matters. A fact I believe I expressed rather tactfully in my carefully crafted response: "Yeah? So what?"

It was then that Sue initiated me into a ancient and holy order: "So this, smart guy: It could be the baby coming." A hasty trip to the doctor's office confirmed that what Freud said about cigars holds true for indigestion: "Sometimes a gas pain is just a gas pain." But driving home from the doctor's office, I was a man obsessed.

"So, is that the big mystery of labor pain? Gas? You mean every time I load up on tamales and refried beans, I share with women everywhere the precious experience of bringing new life into the world? Don't you think men ought to be told this fact? Huh? Don'cha? Maybe you've said too much, honey. I don't want you to get in trouble with the worldwide network of women or anything. Just blink twice if it's a go on this gas thing."

The love of my life turned to face me, turned so slowly that hours seemed to pass. She explained things to me with great patience, or at least with as much patience as a woman who is nine months pregnant can muster, which is not very much patience at all.

Apparently, the onset of labor, the overture, if you will, to the great symphony of agony that follows, can sometimes feel like gas pains. But true labor is nothing like gas pains. Labor is like nothing else in all this wicked world and I, as a mere male (and not a very bright one at that) can never hope to understand.

I'm no stranger to pain. I shattered my left elbow into a zillion pieces a few years ago.

And once, my gall bladder tried to kill me, and we had to take it out and shoot it. But I'm forever to be kept in the dark about this life-bestowing pain. Shucks.

II. GOD IS MY COPILOT; BRUCE SPRINGSTEEN IS THE IN-FLIGHT ENTERTAINMENT.

At 3 a.m. on Sept. 17 — a date that will be known in our family as "Sam's Birthday"— Sue, not about to be given the old sleeping-oaf brush-off again, woke me with the words, "It's time." As I stumbled around, getting ready, I said, "It's a good thing I'm still asleep; otherwise, I might be really nervous."

This was my last joke of the day.

Fifteen years and three kids with the same woman–you pick up a few things. You might be surprised to learn that my witty banter and sparking repartee do not translate well into the whole labor/delivery room milieu. But it's true.

We get in the car: Bruce is on the tape deck, singing about hard roads and mean streets. In the dark, in the rain, Sue and I go to make love real, to turn holy passion into flesh and bone.

Lights out in the labor room

Part 2 of 4 - Sam says "Hi!"
Time travel made easy; or, why the 19th century stunk.

WHEN HOSPITAL PERSONNEL GREET YOUR ARRIVAL at their darkened establishment in the middle of the night with the words, "There is absolutely nothing to worry about. The back-up generators should be kicking in any minute now," well, it's not a good sign.

On the cusp of having our fourth child, Sue and I were whisked up to the labor room in the midst of a hospital-wide power failure. The darkness was the result, we were told, of a highly technical snafu involving, if I remember correctly, "electrical thingies going kerblooey."

Sure enough, no sooner were we settled in our room, when the back-up generators did indeed go to work. Unfortunately, they continued to back up right on out of the hospital and then caught a cab for parts unknown, leaving us with no fetal monitor, no lights and no TV (Merciful God in heaven: anything but that!).

Nurses began scurrying around with flashlights, peering into birth canals like so many coal miners wondering what happened to that darn canary. Suddenly gripped with the fear we'd been transported 150 years into the past, I feared the birth of my fourth son would unfold like an old episode of "Gunsmoke."

Marshal Dillon would take charge: "Somebody boil some water. Festus, go sober up the doc, and get some clean sheets from Miss Kitty's place. (As if the type of establishment Miss Kitty ran was a veritable fount of clean linen.) I reckon this little gal is fixin' to have her young'un right here."

Luckily, at about 9 a.m., the lights came on again and we were all returned to the 20th century.

The back-up generators, though, are still missing. They were last seen headed south on the Garden State Parkway. If you have any information about their whereabouts, let me know so I can tell the hospital.

It was about this time that the miracle of childbirth took a hard left into that cul-de-sac of bad nastiness that many male-type birthing partners know so well. We know we've arrived there because, from this point on in the process, nothing we do is right.

Susan was in throes of something called back labor, a condition I had heretofore associated exclusively with migrant farm workers. She would look at me with eyes full of tender, pleading love: "Honey, could you please rub my back with those strong yet sensitive fingers of yours?"

"Of course, sweetheart," I'd reply. And the minute I began massaging her, I would hear in a voice that was almost-but-not-quite human, "Get those stubby digits away from me, fool!"

Now, back in the days when, as Sue puts it, I was really too stupid to live, I admit that I would take umbrage at that sort of abuse.

But believe me, that sort of thing can become counter-productive pretty quickly. So this time, I just did as she asked and shut up.

At the same time that Sue was having back labor, she was also experiencing contractions. She let me know that. She let the nurses know that. She let strangers passing by in the hallway know that. But the nurses at first refused to acknowledge her genuine and ancient pain, because the machine that monitors contractions didn't register it.

Today, crying out in agony doesn't count for beans if the machine doesn't record it. And so in a time of unparalleled technological advances, it is still true there are "none so blind as those who refuse to see ..."

While she labored, I…ate

Part 3 of 4 - Sam says "Hi!"
The doctor makes an appearance.

ALL THINGS CONSIDERED, it was probably not the best idea to leave my laboring wife's side to go get lunch. But I was hungry.

I also thought I had the time. Sue continued to have contractions throughout the long morning that she struggled to give birth to our fourth son. The machine that was supposed to record the contractions was still on the fritz, though. The doctor – a man who, to the best of my knowledge, has never personally experienced even one contraction in his life – popped in every 20 minutes to examine the ticker tape.

"Well, Mrs. Riley," he'd said, "these contractions don't look so bad."

Despite Sue's polite insistance that she was in real pain, the doctor, operating under the impression that your typical contraction is no more serious than the aftermath of three bad tacos, insisted that my wife (already a mother of three, remember), was mistaken. He persisted in this belief even as the fetal monitor showed a precipitous decline in our baby's heart rate after each "nonexistent" contraction. Finally, around 11 a.m. the doctor said, "OK, Mrs. Riley. What we're gonna do is give you an epidural and dose of a medicine that will regulate these so-called contractions of yours."

The administering of an epidural has always been my cue to leave the proceedings. So, knowing that I had to keep my strength up to be the most supportive birthing partner I could be, I went out for a bite to eat.

A fervent prayer is prayed.

Admittedly, lunch took longer than expected.

Owing to a power failure the night before, the hospital cafeteria staff was attempting to fire up the grill by rubbing two sticks together. So, it was a good 20 minutes before I strolled casually back up to the labor room. I opened the door onto a scene of carnage reminiscent of certain scenes from the movie "Alien."

Unbeknownst to me, the doctor skipped the epidural, and went right to the labor-intensifying medicine. In Sue's case this move caused the whole process to pick up steam. Yes, things were moving at quite a clip.

A nurse pushed me into the bathroom to change into a hospital gown. When I came out, Susan was screaming, the nurses were shouting and the doctor was…lecturing my wife.

"I understand, Mrs. Riley, that this delivery is unlike your others," he said patronizingly. "But we have a fetal heart rate that's all over the place and you really need to get a grip."

"Pull yourself together and listen to me!" he said.

I looked at Susan, who was looking at the doctor. It was then that I prayed harder than I've ever prayed in my life: "Please, dear God, don't let Sue kill the doctor!"

God is good. He answered my prayer. Sue didn't try to kill the doctor. She tried to kill me.

Suddenly, all her years with the World Wrestling Federation came to the fore and my wife grabbed me in some hammerlock death-grip, cutting off blood and oxygen to my vital organs. The nurses pried her loose and told me they would be wheeling Sue to the delivery room "like bats out of hell." This they did, although I doubt bats on the lam from Hades would have run over my foot with the gurney.

Born into a world of dangers

The conclusion - Sam says "Hi!"
Cannon to the left of him, cannon to the right of him.

SOMEWHERE BETWEEN THE LABOR ROOM AND THE DELIVERY ROOM, our doctor disappeared. He was gone. Vanished. I suspect, having seen the homicidal glint in my darling's eyes, he feared for his life and was, at that very moment, frantically calling the Justice Department in an attempt to procure a spot in the Witness Protection Program. Another doctor showed up and tried to look nonchalant about the whole OB-GYN switcheroo. But, hell, by this time Sue and I would not have cared if a circus clown had dropped by to oversee the delivery.

And then, at 11:49 a.m. on Sept. 17, amid much pain and many tears, Samuel Kenan Riley, the most beautiful baby in the world, was born. And by "the most beautiful baby in the world," I don't mean that subjective flapdoodle that most new parents blather on about. I mean that by any objective standard you can name, my newest son is the most beautiful baby in the world.

I'm an expert in the field. I remain firm in my general belief that newborn babies, including my own progeny, are among the ugliest, most scary-looking of all God's creatures. But baby Sam is different. He is the physical manifestation of the Platonic Ideal of newborn beauty.

Any of you got a problem with that? I thought not.

Once Sam was severed from the Mother Ship, so to speak, the nurse whisked him away to the center of a round examination table about three feet in diameter off to my left where he was poked, prodded and suctioned within an inch of his very brief life. I kept one eye on my beautiful Susan and one eye on Sam. I watched his little arms and legs twitch in the center of the white circular table and, suddenly, I noticed all around the perimeter of the table, not 10 inches away from my kid, all manner of knives, scissors and assorted sharp objects. I think I even saw a couple of grenade launchers in there. I was about to run over and snatch my kid away from these obviously deranged hospital people when I realized that Sam, unable to roll and crawl at the age of approximately 2 minutes, was perfectly safe.

But now that I think about it, that baby table is as apt a metaphor for my children's arrival in this veil of tears as I've ever seen.

Our babies come to us safe in the pure white circle of our love for them. But never far away is a dangerous and sin-filled world. We hold our babies for as long as we can, and we pray hard that when heartache and darkness come, we will have given them life and light enough to make their way in the world and to make their way home.

My son: Strange or genius?

MY SECOND-BORN SON, CHRISTOPHER, IS SERIOUSLY WEIRD.

But I'm OK with that. Really. Strange is good. Among other things, I can always offer his quirkiness as proof of my paternity. Besides, it's usually not that big a deal.

In much the same way you tend not to notice that your Uncle Wally yodels when your family bows in prayer at Thanksgiving because, well, it's Uncle Wally, and Uncle Wally has always yodeled during grace, I tend not to notice that my boy is a few bubbles shy of plumb.

But every once in a while, the child will remind me how far from normal he truly is.

This is the kid who, when he was 3, walked into a room full of adults while whacking himself on the noggin with a shoe and said: "You know, I believe there's somebody walking on my head," before calmly stepping out of the room.

A few years later he was the sort of child who could answer any question, a regular oracle at Delphi in a "Batman" T-shirt. If, for instance, you wanted to know how many angels could dance on the head of a pin, he was your man.

"Fifty-six," he might reply. "But only if it's a slow dance," he might add, with such a note of authority that you were suddenly sure all those times he spent staring off into space were not idle moments at all, but rather visions and visitations from the Almighty Himself.

Christopher, who has just turned 13, spent a week in July at a Baptist summer camp. Personally, I think the Dark Ages taught us all we need to know about the risks attendant upon large numbers of fervent young believers being thrust together in pastoral settings. You're just asking for trouble.

It was hard to get the bread baked or the wine pressed down at the local medieval convent or monastery when the nuns and monks were whirling around in a sort of holy fit brought on by mass religious hysteria.

We don't generally have that sort of trouble at the local Baptist summer camp. A daily ration of bug juice and 'smores tends to take the edge off your more lurid apocalyptic visions. And a few choruses of "Kum-By-A" around the evening campfire is enough to prevent nightmares of hellfire (and cure insomnia, to boot).

Nonetheless, all that bucolic scenery and Christian theology must have caused Christopher to miss the on-ramp of the "Normal Expressway."

I picked him up at camp on a bright Saturday morning. On the drive home, I asked him what was the most fun thing he did at camp.

"Well, Dad," he said, "one afternoon, I was in a field by myself and pretended to be dead so that when the buzzards started circling around me, I could jump up and fool them."

Could any parent be more proud? The fruit of my loins aspires to be a carrion decoy, pulling practical jokes on birds, his stated goal in life vis-a-vis buzzards being to "mess with their heads."

The boy is a loon.

Or perhaps, as they say, corpselike waters run deep. Christopher might have been re-enacting the great Christian drama of the New Testament, wherein death is defeated amid great joy and resurrection. My son could be an artist, a saint and a genius all rolled into one.

Either way, I'm making sure he sits next to Uncle Wally next Thanksgiving.

Life's hurts lead us to God's love

THE LAST THING ANY 9-YEAR-OLD BOY NEEDS is a permanent booger hanging from the end of his nose. It's the sort of thing that tends to wear on a guy.

Because it's not just well-meaning adults whispering in your ear that maybe you should wipe your nose. That you can deal with.

But other 9-year-olds? Now there's major trouble. One at a time, they can be little darlings: cute and sensitive and down right teary when Bambi's mother gets it between the eyes. But you get a group of them together, and the local playground turns into the African veldt. And prepubescents become a pack of wildebeests on the hunt.

Woe betide any little boy with a permanent booger hanging from the end of his nose: He's a slow gazelle; he's lunch. There is the scent of weakness in the air, and blood. No amount of rational explanation will stay the baring of teeth, the rending of flesh, the bestowing of moronic nicknames. ("Snotface! Boogerboy!") Childhood can be a hard world and a cruel one, one in which the mark of Cain becomes not a sign of protection and grace, but a bright red bulls' eye.

It seemed as though my boy Alex just woke up one morning with this cyst at the edge of his right nostril, a stalactite of skin hanging from the end of his schnozz. And, from a distance, it did look for all the world like a dollop of petrified snot.

Alex bore his burden well for a time. He tried joking with the kids who taunted him, but I could see the hurt in his eyes. And when the adults would come and hand him a tissue to wipe his nose, he'd stare at the ground and say, very quietly, "No, thank you. It's a cyst."

I think it was those downcast eyes that came closest to breaking my heart. I knew that face, and those eyes. I grew up watching my father looking down, his face always in shadow, a mixture of shame and failure playing over his unblemished features. I hated that face on the man I loved. And I swore early on in this life that it would not become my face. I would hold my head up. I would look a man in the eye no matter what.

Now, a generation removed, my sweet boy was shamed by his own cells. His mother and I worked as quickly as we could to get the blasted thing removed from our boy's nose, which turned out not to be very quickly at all.

We live in a time of HMOs and managed care, meaning that unless you're gut-shot, you're not going to see a doctor without completing a complicated daisy chain of forms and referrals. Days stretched into weeks, and "Soon, sweetheart," was all we could say to Alex, "someday soon, the doctor will fix you up."

Finally, one day in late September, his mother took him to the dermatologist's office. The doctor gave my son a choice of having the cyst burned off or frozen off. Once Alex heard that the freezing thing would take days to work and mean a greater chance of the booger coming back, he was adamant: "Fry the sucker!" A brief crackling of electric fire, an instant of blinding pain and Alex was free again to look up.

The Bible doesn't have a lot to say about ice, but God seems to have a special place in his heart for desert people. So the images of holiness in Scripture are images of conflagration: burning bushes, blazing angels, and refining fires. We've all got something – boogers, cysts, secrets, sins growing in us, holding us down and holding us back. The healing of God hurts like hell, maybe, but it's a healing that lasts forever.

Sons play out ancient roles

Sometimes, I can hear Cain and Abel going at it in the bedroom upstairs, loud and violent. Other times, I watch Jacob and Esau huddled and scheming in the living room, and I know that one of them is getting screwed out of something valuable. Most nights, around the supper table, it's bedlam as Joseph and his brothers fight for territory and their parents' love. And once in a blessed while in my house, I witness Jesus himself reaching out tenderly for a brother in pain.

My sons play out these tales of blood and mystery all the time, and they are a source of wonder to me. In the course of a single day, I see Abel get the upper hand for once over the murderous Cain, and by lunch, Abel changes to the dull-witted Esau, until late at night, when he becomes Joseph, living large down in Egypt land.

Take my son Christopher. At 15, he is an older and younger brother at the same time, and he is quicksilver, changing shape and shedding skin as circumstances demand.

One night not long ago, his older brother, Joshua, asked Christopher to do the dishes for him.

"Please, Chris," Josh said. "I'm tired."

Christopher sat up in his chair like some long-ago potentate

"What will you give me if I do the dishes for you?" Christopher asked. Joshua missed the hint of cruelty just behind his brother's smile.

Uh-oh, I thought to myself, watching from a distance, there's trouble coming

"I'll give you these two CDs," said Joshua, a guy who, under certain circumstances, would sell his birthright for a mess of pottage.

Christopher took the CDs from Joshua's hand, and studied them carefully. Then he turned to look at me.

"Dad," he asked, "Do you know why I'm looking at these CDs?"

"No," I lied.

"I wanted Josh to think for one brief moment that I was actually considering doing the dishes," Chris said. Then he laughed.

And, God forgive me, so did I.

"Why do you have to be such a jerk?" Josh yelled, angry and embarrassed.

He stomped off to the kitchen, where we heard cutlery slamming into the sink, and dishes rattling together like they were on a shelf at a small diner next to the railroad tracks.

"I thought that went rather well," Christopher said, more to himself than to me.

The next day, after school, Christopher and younger brother Alex found themselves home alone. Alex seemed down, and Christopher asked him what was the matter.

It turned out that some kid in the playground had called Alex, in what passes for sixth-grade repartee, "a retard and a fag."

"Don't worry about it," Chris said.

He went to his loose-leaf binder and wrote a note, ripped it out and handed it to Alex.

"Hey, kid," the note read, "You've known my brother for a week, and you don't know jack. Alex is smarter than you and more secure in his heterosexuality than you'll ever be. Alex's brother, Chris. P.S. I'm a WHOLE lot bigger than you."

You would have thought that Alex had been healed of leprosy or that the king had given him safe passage throughout the realm. His smile was huge.

"Thank you, Chris," Alex said.

I grew up in a home without brothers or sisters and was frightened, years later, when I found out that I was going to be a father more than once. The complex interplay of blood and family and love and loathing seemed beyond my ability to comprehend, let alone manage.

Management is out of the question, but I have come to see my family as a grace-fired crucible in which my boys become men in a God-made world where everyone is their brother or sister.

Two bulls, no peace

I CAN'T GIVE THE BOY WHAT HE WANTS.

And he believes, down in his gut, that if he gave me what I wanted, it would take a little piece of his soul. We can't even look at each other these days without fire in our eyes and thunder in our voices. The air between us smells like ozone, a storm always coming.

My son is 17. We named him Joshua when he made his blood-red bawling way into this world. But I watch him now, sneaking a glance in the mirror as he walks down the hallway, and I see Absalom, the son of David, a boy who loved his father . . . and hated him enough to wage war against him.

What he wants, of course, is the freedom to make a damned fool of himself, to screw up and screw around. I try to tell Joshua that he'll have that terrible gift before he knows it, but for now, he's got to wait.

"I can't wait to get out of this house and away from you," he says.

I believe he's one smart-assed comment away from some sort of Outward Bound program, up to his knees in mud and living on tree bark and beetles for a few weeks.

"You should have stopped with one kid," he says sometimes to his mother, meaning we should have stopped with him, because then life would be good for the young prince. But no, we heedlessly brought brothers and rivals into his life, making his circumstances hard and poor.

"Oh, I don't know, Josh," I tell him. "Maybe we should have started with number two."

It always begins like that, in petulance and ridicule, until it turns into something else, something nasty and mean, something that carries within it a hint of menace and the threat of violence.

We see it coming, this fuse burning its way into some gasoline-soaked warehouse, but neither one of us makes a move to save the day or run for cover. Blindness brings a kind of stubborn inevitability into our world.

Once, not long ago, my boy and I were fighting over some undone household job.

We were raising the stakes all the time.

"Why don't you do it," he said. "I never see you lift a finger around here."

Suddenly, I was an inch from his face, roaring at him, calling him an ingrate and worse.

He never flinched, his hands at his side became fists. He's a strong kid, with wiry muscles and speed. I've got bulk and 17 years of holding his hand, wiping his butt and loving him on my side. It's an even match.

The rest of the family was transfixed, a frozen tableau, waiting somehow for permission to move, to breathe, to come back to life again.

Joshua looked at me with disgust and left the room.

It was Sue who spoke first.

"If you ask me," she said, "I think there's entirely too much testosterone in this house."

I spoke with a family therapist later in the week for a story I was working on. Since I had her on the phone, I asked her what the deal was between my first born and me. She had a variation on the testosterone theory.

"No smart farmer," she said, "puts two bulls in the same field."

I can't fault those observations, but I believe the divide between Josh and me, even during the periods where there seems to be an uneasy peace between us, is deeper than chemicals stewing in some primitive part of the brain, and firing their way into words and clenched fists.

There's something spiritual at work. And it's too easy to call it sin and be done with it.

There's grace here, too, and a dark blessing, as father and son each try to be bound by love and freed from other chains at one and the same time.

It'll be wonderful, if we survive this hard time.

Making Dad very proud

PERHAPS I'VE BEEN A LITTLE REMISS, having never instructed my sons in the manly art of fisticuffs. To my credit, though, my boys can do a mean comedy spit-take with a mouthful of water. It's all a matter of priorities.

I've spent most of my life, with remarkable success, avoiding the whole "kick butt or get your butt kicked" business. This was no easy task for some one who grew up in the "Lord of the Flies" environment of a South Jersey trailer park. Bespectacled, chubby and shy, you'd have thought that I would have been the geeky pinata that no group of neighborhood ruffians can do without.

Actually, I was bit of a legend among the toughs.

"Hey, Webster," one of them would call to me, "tell us a big word."

I'd walk over to them like some Old Testament prophet who understands that words have power, the sunlight hitting my glasses, making it look as if my eyes were on fire. I'd say something like, "You guys are looking pretty malevolent today."

"Man, you're just like the Webster's dictionary," they'd say. "Now go away."

See, it was apparently bad mojo to beat up on the guy who knew all the words.

Later on, in high school, it was humor that saved me.

By the time I hit college, everybody was usually too "mellowed out" to be overly aggressive. And then, you're an adult, where, presumably, the Three Stooges Method of Conflict Resolution is generally frowned upon.

So, when it came time to teach my boys to fight, I had nothing to give them.

Besides, some things are best learned on the mean streets.

Not long ago, my 15-year-old son, Christopher, had a baptism of fire. It was one of the those high-noon-under-the-flagpole, back-against-the-schoolyard-wall moments. Called out by a bully, for reasons so murky that they could best be described as Kafkaesque, my son had reached a point where no spit-take would help and even the word "antidisestablishmentarianism" was useless.

Chris is not what you'd call an imposing figure, unless tall, thin, goofy and gawky is your idea of an imposing figure.

Nowhere to run to, nowhere to hide, my son stepped into the arena, ready to defend both himself and what's left of the tattered Riley honor.

By most accounts, he cleaned the kid's clock.

And he became a hero to the weak and oppressed, and a beloved outlaw even to the authorities who brought him in.

At home, I watched Chris as he told the story, an adrenalin buzz still in his voice hours later. He at least looked like he could take a punch or two.

As a parent, particularly a parent of the "Be like Jesus and Always Turn the Other Cheek" variety, I faced something of a quandary: On the one hand, I wanted to tell him that he'd done wrong. On the other hand, the kid's got a helluva right jab.

Of course, Christ himself was known to go medieval on the occasional money-changer in the Temple. Nevertheless, I fear my heart-to-heart with my boy sounded sort of schizophrenic: "That was terrible! Way to go, boy!"

Which is sort of how they treated him in the stir after he was suspended.

It's a "zero tolerance for violence" sort of world in school these days, and self-defense is no defense at all. And that's the way it should be.

But in the midst of exile, Chris heard that what he'd done, although intolerable, might have done the community some sort of good. Like Batman's brand of vigilante justice.

Chris remains humble, like a gunslinger hanging up his holster.

"I've got nothing to prove," he says. "I'm a peaceable sort."

That, of course, is his true strength and courage and power. It makes me proud.

A father's tears in the Jersey heat

SOME TEARS ARE HARD TO TAKE. Little boys, for instance, don't like to see their daddies cry.

A father's tears can make children more frightened than the bogeyman who rises every night from the pile of dirty socks and T-shirts in the hamper, scratching, growling and muttering dark threats from behind the closet door. Because even a little kid knows that the bogeyman is not real, at least not real in the way Mommy's arms are real when they hold him while she banishes the bogeyman with a sweet song.

A father's tears are too real for a child. You can see them stain his cheeks, get stuck in the stubble of his beard. A little boy knows where the bogeyman comes from: he comes from the hamper in the closet. But where would his father's tears come from? There is neither blood nor bruise on him, no scraped knee nor bruised noggin, no booboo at all on his big body.

Not knowing where those tears come from is scary enough. More frightening still is the little boy's realization that there may not be any arms strong enough, nor any songs sweet enough, to stop his father's tears.

One summer day five years ago, I scared the bejabbers out of my oldest son. The Rileys had come from their home in Massachusetts to spend a week at summer camp in New Jersey. Four and a half Rileys had made their way 300 miles in a maroon Dodge Aries that was in the throes of such a massive mechanical depression it periodically would just up and stop. "I'm just a worthless hunk of junk," our car would say to us as it sputtered down the Connecticut Turnpike. "You'd be better off without me."

Medication and kind words

While we all secretly agreed, we would nurse the car along, encourage it, feed it massive doses of 10w40, the Thorazine of the automotive set, saying, "Buck up! You can make it. All you need is a good tune up and a change of scenery."

Not many days after we ended this ill-fated journey, our car committed suicide in our driveway. It left a note: "Save the tires." To this day, I think the trip to New Jersey had a lot to do with its decision.

It was hot that July at camp in New Jersey, that stinky, sticky kind of hot New Jersey does so well. The kind of heat that causes bugs and mosquitoes to mutate into huge blood-sucking beasts. The kind of hot that hell must get on a very bad day. As a matter of fact, I believe that when the fallen angels were setting up shop in hell, Satan must have said to a few of his demons, "Listen, I hear they're doing great things with misery and suffering up in Jersey. Check it out. We could use some tips."

There was a lake at camp in which one presumably could take a refreshing dip, if one did not mind having to do battle with the Giant Algae Monster that had taken it over. The choice was between being hot enough to fry eggs on your stomach or being cool but slime-covered.

It was not a choice I had to make because, not many weeks before, I had broken my elbow in a fall at church. Shattered it, really. They had to take a piece of my hip to make me a new elbow. At the time of our stay in camp, I had this thing on my arm, a cast the doctors called it, but it was really an ingenious torture device. It had two settings: unbearable itching and interminable pain.

Susan had problems of her own, not the least of which was being eight months pregnant. There is nothing quite like finishing up a pregnancy in the dog days of summer. The special radiance that attends women who are with child really takes on a freakish glow in the summer. She was big and miserable. It looked like our third child had set up a Taco Bell in the womb. The circulation in her legs was on the fritz; she huffed and puffed up and down the hills at camp. And she frequently would shoot me baleful glances as if this whole pregnancy thing was somehow my fault.

But we're a hardy bunch, we Rileys. We can take it. Bad car, bum elbow, tough pregnancy, horrible climate. Bring it on. No sweat. (Well, OK, there was sweat.) No problem. We're tough . . . Then, not two days into our Club Gehenna Vacation, my 3-year-old son Chris, never the most agile of children, tripped over a blade of grass or a gum wrapper or some darn thing and sprained his ankle, which meant he had to be carried everywhere by someone – his one-armed dad or his Earth mother mom.

We had become a family of refugees, shell-shocked and battle-scarred, on the lam from life itself. We hobbled around wondering where we could go to find a little scrap of peace. I had had it. On Thursday, right after lunch, I sat down on my lower bunk and cried.

I cried over the stupid heat, my stupid car, my stupid elbow, my stupid pregnant wife, my stupid gimpy kid, and the stupid God who presumably had let all these things happen to us without lifting one of His omnipotent fingers to help. I thought I was alone, but Joshua, who was 5, stuck his head in the doorway and saw me.

"Don't cry"

He was spooked. "Daddy, don't cry," he said. But he wasn't saying it to comfort me. He was ordering me to stop.

"Daddy, don't cry" meant "MAYDAY! MAYDAY! We're going down in flames! The planet has slipped loose from its moorings and is flying out of the Milky Way! The center cannot hold! If you lose it, what chance have I got to save my 5-year-old soul in this world? Knock it off!"

I knocked it off for his sake.

Confession may be good for the soul, but hearing confessions is just terrifying. And not just for 5-year-olds, either. Getting something off your chest is all well and good, but most of us don't want to have to handle stuff from somebody else's chest.

Even the apostles didn't want to hang around when Jesus confessed His weakness in a flood of tears and sweat in the Garden of Gethsemane. "Stay with me," Jesus said. And the disciples took a nap.

When someone we expect to be strong and pure tells us he is scared or angry or sad, we are shaken. I see the fear sometimes when I tell stories about who I am and where I've fallen: "Tell God, but don't tell me."

Sometimes we need to tell our tales or shed our tears not before God in heaven, but before the God who shines through our brothers and sisters in faith. We need God to have a face, sometimes, and arms to hold us and songs to sing to us.

Any idiot can cry. And most of us do. And all of us have good reason to. To grow up in faith, though, means to let God give you the loving strength to hear the worst about someone you care about from his own lips. And not be afraid. And not turn away. God may heal you both in wondrous ways.

We all need blankets to stay warm

MY THIRD SON ALEX LOVES JESUS and Mom and Daddy and his brothers and Grandmom and Pop Pop and, on good days, "everybody in the whole world."

But if he ever were up against it and forced to choose between the continued existence of this wild and fragile world and his "blanky," well, let's just say I think Jesus and all the rest of us would be flat out of luck. Alex really, really loves his blanket.

Greenblanket. One word. Because there is no other blanket.

Oh, sure, there are things people use to keep warm at night, but they are pale imitations of the One True Blanket. Some of them may even look green to the untrained eye, but Alex is not fooled. There is one greenblanket in all of creation – and it's his.

From the cradle and through all five of his years on this earth, the greenblanket has been by his side. It's been bled on, pooped on, thrown up on, drooled on, spat on. It has survived and helped Alex get through long feverish nights and thunderstruck days. It's there when Mom and Dad are asleep and Jesus is out to lunch. The greenblanket, unlike some parents he could name, asks nothing of him, makes no demands on him, never yells at him.

He will grow old with this thing, will read its color by touch if he goes blind. He will die in his ancient bed with it, be buried with it. He will lug it forever around Heaven with him. And if Jesus plays His cards right, Alex may let Him borrow it once in a while, because even the Lamb of God has a bad day now and again.

After lunch these days, I drive Alex to kindergarten. Just before we get in the car, he will say, "Wait a minute, Dad." He will run to the greenblanket, rub it against his cheek a half-dozen times and, thus fortified, sally forth to do battle with the forces of public education.

One morning last week, my son's blanket carried me to holy ground, to a space aflame with the sacred. Heaven got quiet, and time itself was wrapped in the grandeur and mystery of the Almighty.

"You know, Dad," Alex said to me, "sometimes I talk to my greenblanket."

It seemed an easy thing for him to say. Too easy. For just a second, a look of fear passed in his eyes. He had said too much, gotten weak and shot off his mouth.

If I so much as smiled too broadly, something terrible would happen. Something between us would be lost, maybe forever. I could hear the rustle of angels' wings around me. Even the hosts of Heaven were nervous, afraid I would somehow profane this moment.

On holy ground, secrets are revealed. We kneel barefoot and baresouled before the burning bush, and God Himself tells us His hidden name.

My son, 5 years old, an unholy terror most of the time, had said something to me that he had not spoken to another living soul. Not his brothers, not the woman who had borne him, not even God. He had no choice now but to hope his Dad was up to the task.

I couldn't ignore his words, although that might have gotten us both off the hook. Holy ground is not be dismissed. I couldn't laugh: laughter might have broken us both. This was serous business.

I lowered my head ever so slightly, acknowledging the Father of us both, the Father of us all. I looked my boy in the eye. In this new place, we were equals. I spoke slowly, in a quiet voice that was not a whisper. In this holy time, we were not ashamed.

"What do you say to your blanket, Alex?"

The room we were in shuddered some. It might have been the rumble of a passing train. It might have been the Almighty shifting in His throne.

Alex smiled. It was his turn, and he could afford to smile. The holy place held. The burning bush did not burn out.

"I just tell it when I'm coming home, that I miss it and that it makes me comfortable."

And then, because none of us can stand the holy for too long, I started us home: "You know Alex, some day you won't need your green blanket."

"I know that, Dad. And you know how I know that? Because you always tell me that," Alex said, all mock indignation.

We were all the way home. But like Moses, we had been changed by the Lord. Alex's idol, made of cloth, not stone nor wood, had become a sacred channel of grace. Alex knew now that trust is real and that faith brings blessings. I know what it means to be blessed.

Funerals & Weddings

The bar is their church

SO, THIS BARTENDER WALKS INTO A CHURCH . . .

Well, OK, he didn't exactly walk into the church, what with him being dead and all; and technically, I suppose, you could make the case that he wasn't actually in the church, since his sister had his body cremated and whisked down to some family plot in Florida before his friends and customers even realized that "Buddy" had been called up to that Big Taproom in the Sky. (NO COVER, NO MINIMUM, PERPETUAL HAPPY HOUR!)

But Buddy was there at my church on that Sunday afternoon not long ago when those who had known him and who, in their own hard way, had loved him, gathered to say good-bye. He was there in spirit, as we say, and he was there in spirits as well, the distilled and courage-inducing kind, which a goodly number of the mourners had imbibed a goodly amount of before the memorial service.

I had gotten a call from a woman who had known the deceased, and was close to Buddy's girlfriend. She told me about Buddy's untimely passing, and the sister's speedy disposition of his remains. She said that all the bartender's friends were lost now, left without a way to bid farewell to the man who had, in so many ways (well, mostly one way), eased their pain. She used the word "closure" a lot. Could I please officiate at a memorial service at my church? "Just an informal service. Most of the people who'll show up don't usually go to church – the bar is really their church," she said.

I said yes, because I am, after all, a minister of the gospel, and because of all the Baptist joints in all the towns in the world, they had picked mine. That must mean something, I kept thinking to myself, never imagining for a moment what it might mean is I had finally slipped over the line into full-blown insanity. I kept my Sunday suit on after the morning's worship service, and, in the middle of the afternoon, I unlocked the front door of the church.

They came. About two dozen of them. A few of them hung onto something like quiet dignity, but most of them looked around the church as if at any moment God himself would burst through the door and thunderbolt their sorry butts to hell. Which says something about the courage it took for most of them to show up in this place. You really had to admire them. This was not easy for them in all kinds of ways that had nothing at all to do with the grief they must have felt. I had no idea what any of them thought about Jesus. They'd probably bumped into him now and again, glimpsed him through their fogs on the night before, felt him flogging their temples on the morning after. That water into wine trick might have impressed them a little, but not as much as if Jesus had been able to turn a little water into a fifth of Jack.

One guy on his way to a pew dropped to his knees and genuflected wildly, the way he remembered doing it when he was a kid. There was liquor on the breath of some of them. I'd expected that. What surprised me was that a few of them seemed to be seeping alcohol through their pores, which then condensed into small clouds just above their heads.

They came. The rummies, the alkies, and the barflies. Young women came, looking for all the world like B-girls on the Warner Brothers back lot along about 1940. Older women were there as well, bearing in the lines of their faces every dumb move and bad break life had handed them.

I stood behind the pulpit waiting for them to settle in. And suddenly, I had a sense that the circus had come to town, a sad and lonely Circus of the Damned, to be sure, but a circus nonetheless. I was trapped in a movie: Chaucer's Canterbury Tales as directed by Frederico Fellini. But "where two or three are gathered in my name, there I am in the midst of them," Jesus said.

I prayed that He be there somewhere and began the funeral.

Of funerals, booze and hysteria

THERE ARE PEOPLE IN THIS WORLD for whom every moment carries with it the aura of impending disaster. Their eyes are always wide open, looking for trouble, hoping for it, in fact, because as long as you're in trouble, they figure, you're still alive. They know nothing about living lives of "quiet desperation." Their desperation is noisy, reckless and, with a little bit of luck, bloody as hell. Because if you can bleed, you're still alive.

This is the kind of person who came to bid farewell to Buddy the dead bartender at my church one Sunday afternoon not long ago. As funerals go, it was a pretty fine piece of guerrilla warfare – land mines of booze and grief exploding all over the sanctuary, sniper fire from the back pews, the pulpit riddled with tears. And not a foxhole in sight.

I knew that some of these folks would want to deliver eulogies on behalf of the one who would no longer fill their shot glasses. Before the service, one woman was insistent. Her eyes were red from tears, her voice just a little shy of hysteria. "I can do it!" she said. "I can do it!"

She couldn't do it. She didn't get past "I loved Buddy..." before she broke down in great heaving sobs. Great heaving sobs amplified by the microphone and bounced off the walls of the sanctuary. Finally, someone else got up to speak, and she walked back to her seat. "You guys all know me," he said. "And you know how I have money problems. Never have any money for cigarettes. Well, let me tell you what kind of man Buddy was. I'd walk into the bar and not say a word, and Buddy would smile at me and give me some cigarettes."

Well, now, that wasn't so bad, I thought. A quiet anecdote revealing a man's simple generosity. Maybe we'll get through this thing after all.

Then the cowboy got up to speak. Thin, bearded, carrying a weather-beaten hat with a feather in its band, he stood at the pulpit and cleared his throat. "I got something to say," he said. "Been on my mind since I was 6 years old."

Uh-oh, I thought. This could take a while.

It did. I couldn't really follow the gist of his speech, but the ending was delivered in a bellow. "Buddy was there for me when I was 6. He was there for me when I was 18. AND BY GOD HE WAS THERE FOR ME LAST WEEK." The cowboy raised his hat in the air and strode down the center of the sanctuary railing against churches in general, more specifically those churches he'd had to set foot in when he'd buried his three ex-wives, and vowing not to set foot in one again until his sainted mother shuffled off this mortal coil. He barreled out the front of the church in a dramatic snit (and slunk back in not two minutes later).

By this time, the woman who had broken down earlier had regained enough of her composure to literally drag people up to the microphone, pulling at them even after they said they didn't feel up to it. She pulled Buddy's roommate up to mutter a few words about how he missed his friend. She pushed the deceased's girlfriend up the altar to whisper how she wished they'd had more time together. Suddenly, it was my turn. I began to preach the words of hope and comfort I always do, but there was an edge in my voice, something hard in my tone. It was if there were subtitles to my homily: "Will you people straighten up, and get it through your sodden heads that God gives a rip about you." And this woman was at my elbow, tugging my sleeve. In the middle of my sermon. "We have to sing a song for Buddy," she whispered.

"No, we don't," I said. "Really, we don't."

We did. Two stanzas of a cappella Amazing Grace sung by two dozen folks who didn't know the words. But God knows they tried. And in that moment, pathetic and embarrassing, I saw that these people were Christ's people, sad, sick and lonely sinners. He loved them now and forever. And, for just a second or two, so did I.

Lasting marriages require sweat equity

THE GUY DIDN'T WANT TO SWEAT. Perfectly understandable. There are many times when I myself prefer not to sweat. I like that quality in a person. Really. A laudable ambition, not sweating. His desire not to sweat is even more admirable when you consider it was a rented tuxedo in which he didn't want to sweat.

He subscribes to a higher moral standard than I do. I look at pit stains on a rented tux the same way I look at a spilled milkshake on the front seat of a Hertz car: It's regrettable but, hey, it's a rental. As it was later explained to me, whatever this guy's general feelings about perspiring and the ethical obligations inherent in the lessee-lessor relationship, it was his specific intention not to sweat during the late-afternoon hour when he was ushering at his friend's wedding.

And so it was, with a discipline not seen since the more flagellant orders of monks folded during the Dark Ages, our man decided to embark on a course of action designed to stem the tide of perspiration. He fasted. Neither food nor drink would pass his lips until he stood by his friend the groom, until he ushered the last third cousin twice removed from the sanctuary. His heart was pure. His spirit was strong and his spirit was willing. His flesh? Well, his flesh did what flesh is wont to do on hot May afternoons in close quarters. His flesh leaked. He sweated. "Like a gusher," one of the bridesmaids said. And then he fainted.

Sometime between the "I do's" and "O Promise Me," he just went down. I didn't actually see this (although there's probably enough video of it to embarrass him for the rest of his days) because the wedding party was spread out in a flying wedge formation on the altar steps out of range of my peripheral vision, and I was busy concentrating my own leaky flesh and frazzled spirit on uniting the couple before me in holy matrimony.

I look at a wedding ceremony the way Tennyson saw "The Charge of the Light Brigade": Though there be cannon to the left of me, cannon to the right of me, though all around me are dropping like flies, I will plunge on into that dark valley.

Someone ushered out the usher, and we finished the nuptials. It is things like this, though, that convince Jesus and me weddings can be a real pain in the neck. Now don't get us wrong. Marriage is fine. Marriage is great. Jesus recommends it: "What God hath joined together," he says, "let no one put asunder." I even have one. A marriage, I mean. It turned 10 years old this week. I'll admit it takes a little more work than it used to. It's a little rough around the edges, and sometimes you have to jiggle it just right to get it going in the morning. But most days it shines with the splendor of Heaven, and I wouldn't part with it for all the world.

Jesus and I don't even mind going to weddings. There was Jesus, John's gospel tells us, at the wedding feast in Cana (where you can bet not sweating was the least of anyone's worries), scarfing down the crab puffs and making small talk with the bride's Aunt Sadie who flew in from Miami. Wolfing down hors d'oeuvres and schmoozing are two of my best things. It's when you try to get us to do something at weddings, to contribute in some way to the festivities outside of our aforementioned roles as eaters and chatters, that we try to draw the line.

At the wedding feast in Cana, they ran out of wine.

"Make some wine for the nice people," said Mary.

"No way, Ma," Jesus replied. "You know how I feel about these things."

Of course Jesus was a nice Jewish boy who loved his mother, so he did turn the tap water into Dom Perignon. And I will, because I'm a nice Gentile boy with a minister's diploma on my wall, officiate at the things, working what miracles I can with the help of the Holy Spirit.

The problem with weddings is that there is so much beyond the control of the minister. At least at funerals, everybody pretty much stays put. The average wedding today has more movement than a full-blown production of "Swan Lake." You got your badly dehydrated ushers, lamely attempting to divide guests according to bloodlines in flagrant violation of most civil rights legislation. You got your fidgety, runny-nosed nieces and nephews with pillows or flowers getting lost on their way up the aisle. You got bridesmaids, maids of honor and best men, all over the place. You got your shell-shocked parents of the bride and groom not quite knowing where to go or what to do. You got rings being dropped, trains carried, veils lifted, and people sitting, standing and kneeling with as much precision as an aerobics workout. We could have captured Baghdad with less hassle.

Well, some folks say, isn't a wedding a wonderful and exciting ritual, so richly evocative of the spontaneous messiness of life? Seriously deranged people say that. Seriously deranged people who never have been ministers say stuff like that.

A wedding ceremony is like life only if life took place in a dentist's chair with the nitrous oxide going full blast. A nerve-wracked giddiness in uncomfortable shoes that have to be back at the formal wear store before the mall closes is no way for a man and woman to begin a life together.

There is one other difference between a funeral and a wedding that points to a great sadness surrounding the maniacal joy around the rite of marriage. When I perform a funeral service, the deceased tends to stay dead. When I ask a couple if they will love each other until death parts them, the odds are 50-50 they will turn out to have been mistaken when they answer yes.

People do not tend to stay married much anymore, in part because they don't believe Jesus meant what He said about marriage being forever, about two people becoming, strangely and wonderfully, "one flesh." Most couples I marry look at Jesus as a ditzy rich uncle they have to invite to the wedding for the sake of appearance and the fact that they'll probably get a better class of presents.

If they could see Him instead as the One who will abide with them all their days, as the One who will deepen their love and their faith and their lives and their children's lives, as the One who waits to give Himself if but asked, their marriages might stand more than a coin flip's chance of making it.

Even with Christ to drink deeply from, marriage (if not the actual wedding) gives men and women plenty of chances for working up a sweat. There is the hot sweat of passion, there in the marriage bed, a gift from God. There is the cold sweat of fear, as a husband or wife or child falls ill. There is the sweat of making a marriage work when the other partner is impossible or when you are. There is the sad sweat that comes from being left alone too many nights or fed up to here too many days. But with Jesus Christ, we will sweat and not swoon, but mount up like eagles until death does indeed part us.

Does God work cruel miracles?

CHRISTOPHER DANIEL LEO WENT TO HEAVEN THE DAY HE WAS BORN. It was not a long trip, as these journeys go. He lived through three brief, hopeless hours of October 6.

He traveled light and gave everyone the slip, looking for the life he'd been promised, the life he hadn't even had a chance to lose on his own. The doctors couldn't save him. Didn't even try, really. They knew what they were up against, and they knew they were beaten.

I've seen pictures of Christopher. Soft and beautiful, he had it all: 10 little fingers, 10 tiny toes, a perfect face and parents who loved him with all they had. The one thing he did not have was a brain.

What he had instead was a cluster of cells at the top of his spine, firing up his heart and lungs and his legs often enough and well enough to fool everybody into thinking he would grow up and grow old. It was not until two weeks before he was due that doctors discovered this little one's terrible secret.

There are miracles in this world. But some of them are cruel: dark and treacherous wonders that leave your faith wrecked and ruined, your soul lost and wandering. These are the terrible miracles that make you wonder what sort of God would work them, or set you thinking that maybe there is no God at work anywhere in these desolate times.

That Christopher Daniel, made in the image of this maybe-God, hung onto something like life for as long as he did is one of these cruel miracles. His mom and dad cradled him in their arms, kissed him and whispered their love to him. They watched him move and heard him try to breathe. If love alone could have cured him, he would today be cooing and crying, burping and learning to work his lips into a smile.

But neither love, nor magic, nor hope, was enough to heal him. His heartbeat grew fainter, his breathing harder, and he was gone.

I want to know: If our God is going to take credit for making holy men in their mothers' wombs, is He going to take responsibility for this unmade, unfinished little boy? Because Christopher Daniel's problems began way back and deep down in the genes, where enzymes twist and meet and in their connections make brain and blood and bone.

It is just there, where life comes from the nonliving, just at the moment when all flesh responds to the quickening word of God, that something went wrong. Was God so busy numbering the hairs on the boy's head He forgot to give him a brain?

I tell you this as a minister of the Lord Jesus Christ: Believing is hard, hard work. In a world where it all goes wrong so often, it is sometimes hardly possible to keep the faith. I lose God, now and then, in the dark.

"Where is the Lord?" people ask me. I don't know. Yet somewhere on the edge of the world, below the horizon, a light still shines.

One place where the Lord was in the days after Christopher Daniel died was with the child's orphaned parents. He was in the high and holy love Victor and Jeanine feel for each other. He was in every tear they shed, every sad embrace, every word they spoke to one another.

It was Victor and Jeanine who brought God back to me, who led me up to the altar where, in His sanctuary, family and friends gathered in His name to say goodbye to a little boy we would never know.

Loss of a child can only be healed by God

THE BODY AND BLOOD OF CHRIST had to make way for the bits and pieces of a life never lived. I don't think Jesus minded.

On the Communion table sat teddy bears and storybooks. A picture of Christopher Daniel Leo, cradled in his father's arms, stood next to a tiny urn that held an almost impossibly small pile of cremains: ashes to ashes and dust to dust in record time. Victor and Jeanine, a mommy and a daddy for only three hours before their son died because he was born without a brain, had come home from California to bury their child.

I can still see that photograph on the Lord's table. Victor is wearing drab green hospital scrubs. He is standing, awkwardly holding up his son to the camera. Victor is smiling that broad, dopey grin common to all new fathers.

We know that smile; we've smiled that smile. It comes from someplace in us holy and full of hope. A smile for the sheer wonder of being in on making a life. It is a dream smile, a vision of tomorrows: scraped knees and kindergarten, learner's permits and junior proms, heartbreaks and graduations, weddings and grandchildren. Victor knows his son won't be alive when the moon comes up, but he can't stop dreaming, can't help smiling, even while his son turns blue and dies in his arms.

Victor Leo is in the Navy. He has traveled halfway across the world, met King Neptune when he crossed the equator for the first time. But he had already made a more arduous journey years before that. Victor had traveled from Mohammed back 600 years to be born anew in Jesus Christ. That leap from Islam to the Christian faith had cost him plenty: the love of his family, the respect of his friends. All he has to show for it, really, is a wild promise of eternal life made by an itinerant Jewish rabbi who wound up as dead as Victor's newborn son. And Victor found Jeanine.

Jeanine grew up in the church. Her leap of faith was that short hop from the front pew to the baptismal pool. She is a quiet young woman, filled with a hallowed light and dignity. She speaks softly but with power. Jeanine learned about Jesus from her mother, Alice, one of the saints God sends to us every once in a while to show the rest of the world what it means to live and die in the Lord. Alice died two years ago, and Jeanine bore in herself the sad promise of Christ that those who mourn shall be blessed with comfort. She must now ask Jesus to make good on that promise once again, as she prepares to lay her son down in the same dark ground.

Jeanine knows what she doesn't know, and that is more than most people can claim for themselves. Once, in the days after Christopher died, I asked her how she was feeling. "I feel sad," she said, "but I don't know what else I feel."

How could she? What had she to compare this pain with? Her very body had sheltered her son for nine months, kept him warm and safe. Outside her, he was naked and doomed. Into a wisdom born out of ignorance, the Lord begins his sure and healing work.

I'm a cynical man. Sentimentality is a sucker's game as far as I'm concerned. But you look at Victor and Jeanine, and you see two people who are made for each other. They fill each other's empty spaces like no couple I have ever met. When I think of them, of their simple devotion to one another, of their pure love, I ache somehow, long for what they have.

They walked the six flights of stairs to my office. We sat together and planned a funeral. Victor and Jeanine's life had suddenly been filled by their son's death. Filled with all the toys he would never hold, all the songs he would never sing, all the stories he would never hear. We spoke of songs we would sing, and prayers we would pray.

Victor asked haltingly and with difficulty if I would tell the story of Abraham and Isaac during the funeral. Tell how Abraham held the knife above his son's upturned throat, willing to sacrifice the child of laughter and promise for God's sake. This is not the story I would have chosen, and my face must have turned strange. "We don't mean that we have sacrificed our son. We just want to give him freely to our God, who will take care of him for us," Jeanine said in a whisper.

My office is old and leaky. My faith is too, some days. But these two young people fixed me and filled me, gave me the strength to sing and preach a sermon about life and death and love.

I am taking my time telling this story, but some stories are like that.

When a baby dies, only God can help

A GROWN-UP DIES, AND THE WORLD BECOMES A LITTLE BIT SMALLER. Our friend dies, say, or our husband, or our wife, and the circle of who we are contracts. There is one fewer person to join us on our pilgrim way through this world. You hang around long enough, and they all seem to go, leaving you alone in the lifeboat, leaving the world so small you fear you might bump your head on the sky if you try to stand up.

But a child dies, and the world grows large, is filled suddenly with all the songs that will remain unsung, all the promises that will never be kept and all the dreams that will go undreamed. The stars above us move out into the infinite black, the dark ocean churns and expands beneath us, and we don't know if our small boat will ever make landfall.

Funerals are for putting the world right again after death has messed things up for the living. We say we're "making arrangements," and more than arranging a body in a box or a box in the ground, we are arranging the whole damned world, making the world the right size again, making it fit. There is a certain sameness to funerals, a numbing comfort that comes from knowing we've done this before, and we'll do it again before, at last, it's our ending that has set the world awry.

The prayers at a funeral are almost always the same: asking God to be with us, to comfort us, to give us the strength to go on in the days ahead. The dog-eared Bible, out of which we expect to hear God answer us, is nearly always opened to the same passages.

First, the poetry of the Psalms: "Yea, though I walk through the valley of the shadow of death, I will fear no evil." Then the cocky proclamations of the Apostle Paul: "Behold! I show you a mystery. We shall not all die, but we shall all be changed, in a flash, in the twinkling of an eye . . . and the dead shall be raised." And the sweet, hopeful words of Jesus: "In My Father's house are many mansions . . . I go to prepare a place for you."

Even the songs we usually sing are old and familiar: "In the Garden," and "Amazing Grace," "How Great Thou Art" and "The Old Rugged Cross." Dad always loved that song. It was Aunt Ella's favorite.

The preacher, if he's any good, will try to make at least part of any funeral unique. There is a story to tell here about some special one, about good times had. He will call up a life out of the memories of a family or friends. Dad's laugh, the time Mom fell out of the sailboat, the Christmas when we went to the cabin and it snowed, the time Millie came to my house and just let me cry.

But when a baby dies, three hours into this world, what songs are there to sing, what stories are there to tell?

We who gathered started out in the old and familiar ways. We prayed and we heard the psalms and words of comfort from Scripture. Then the soloist stood up and sang out, with a slow and mournful beauty, "He's Got the Whole World in His Hands," changing one verse ever so slightly. "He's got that little baby in his hands," she sang, and we knew it was true.

Then the pianist began playing, with two fingers, a certain song. She played it the way a child would hear it, the way a child would learn it: "Jesus loves me, this I know, for the Bible tells me so. Little ones to Him belong, for they are weak, but He is strong." All was silence, except for the simple melody.

I spoke of fairy tales and once-upon-a-time stories. I imagined a baby freely given to the Lord's safekeeping in a land without tears. Would the angels rock him to sleep? Would Christopher crawl under Heaven's banquet table? Would he grow up in Heaven and grow wise and handsome? It was a story to tell and I hope it was true. Once upon a time, it began, and happily ever after, it ended.

But what of us, choked with grief and blind to grace? How would our stories end? Never mind happily ever after. Would we ever be happy again? We bear witness, and God may yet bless us and deliver us from this sad time.

The pianist sat down at the piano again and played "Jesus Loves Me" with all 10 fingers. We sang a child's song as adults, on our way from once upon a time to happily ever after: "Jesus take this heart of mine, make it pure and wholly Thine. On the cross you died for me, I will try to live for Thee."

In faces broken by grief, voices throaty but strong, I saw people make a promise to God. "I will try..."

"Jesus loves us" is all we have, all we are only sometimes sure of. But it may be enough to bring us all the way home.

Pop Culture
&
Church Life

Hey, moral depravity is popular

FROM THE AUGUST HALLS OF THE UNITED STATES SENATE comes word that American popular culture is a festering sinkhole of moral depravity. And the only reasonable and intelligent response on the part of the citizenry of this great republic must surely be: Well, duh.

American popular culture has always been a festering sinkhole of moral depravity. Benjamin Franklin wrote treatises on breaking wind and keeping mistresses. Mark Twain let Huckleberry Finn smoke that corncob pipe to his heart's content. And the Golden Age of Vaudeville was no church social, that's for sure, what with the laugh riot that ensued when some performer in blackface went all bug-eyed, saying, "Lawdy, Lawdy, I'se shore am in a worl' ob trubb'le now," after getting caught stealing watermelons.

The morally uplifting Chautauqua shows in the early part of this century were attended mostly by folks in the hinterlands who thought that the lecturers on Temperance were just a warm-up act and left feeling cheated when it turned out that there were no can-can girls. If you think I'm being overly cynical here, ask yourself this question: How long did those Chautauqua shows last once the hoi polloi were able to plop a penny in one of them new-fangled movin' pitcher machines and take a gander at "Sweet Marie, Her Fans, and What The Plumber Saw"?

It's not just America, either. The French think that Jerry Lewis is a comic genius, for Pete's sake; and the fact that a goodly number of them are tanked on Beaujolais is no excuse. Japanese game shows make "Wheel of Fortune" contestants look like a gathering of Nobel laureates, and you don't even want to know about their comic books.

Popular culture nearly always appeals to the lowest common denominator; and that includes Shakespeare and Italian opera. Shakespeare always wrote for Joe Sixpack (or Joe "A Few Tankards of Grog," as he was known back in Elizabethan times.) Any of you folks checked out the rape and pillage quotient in Titus Andronicus lately? The Bard of Avon had a mouth on him, too: ol' Bawdy Bard, they called him, what with all his curses, epithets and dirty jokes. (For a partial list, send a self-addressed, stamped envelope to me, care of this newspaper). And don't get me started on opera: Pretty much every time the fat lady sings, you can bet she's caterwauling about sex or violence.

In fact, the only time that mass entertainment doesn't pander to the baser instincts of humanity is when the government commissions it. Then, it's worse. The Communists of the former U.S.S.R. fell out of power not merely because of the savage idiocy of Marxist-Leninist doctrine, but because the people finally got fed up with seventy years of compulsory attendance at dramas with titles like "The Workers' Triumphant Productivity Increase at the Ball Bearing Factory in Irkusk." They do the same thing in the People's Republic of China, but most of the 900 million peasants don't have cab fare to the theater, so I suspect it's going to take a little longer for the old regime to crumble.

Speaking of pandering, and speaking of government, let's talk about Bob Dole for a minute. Earlier this year, he took time from his busy schedule dismantling the Federal bureaucracy and cozying up to every right-wing nutbar with a few bucks to throw his way to deplore the dreck coming out of Hollywood and to review movies that he thought promoted "family values." He did not, however, have the time to actually see the movies he reviewed. He thought, for instance that the Arnold Schwarzenegger flick "True Lies" was a fine little family movie. I've seen it: The last twenty minutes are pretty exciting, but on the whole, the movie is stupid, stupid, stupid. Which family values were promoted? The one where bored and lonely housewives start adulterous affairs? The one where a cuckolded husband forces his wife into a humiliating strip-tease in front of someone she believes to be a total stranger? Or maybe the value wherein mom and dad are committing to blowing away dozens of swarthy Middle Eastern types?

Bob Dole can't tell a festering sinkhole from a hole in the ground. Hollywood makes garbage for the simple reason that garbage sells. People are sinners, and are titillated by the vicarious immorality flickering on the silver screen. It's not Hollywood's job to turn the soul of America to higher things. That's my job. And God's. It's not easy, I'll tell you that: You people will watch anything.

But sometimes a violent, foul-mouthed movie actually raises profound questions of Christian theology, which is what my oldest son and I found out when we went to go see "Pulp Fiction."

There's no accounting for taste

ALL RIGHT, CLASS. Put down that coffee cup, swallow that forkful of scrambled eggs, and repeat after me: "De gustibus non est disputandum." Feels good, doesn't it, wrapping your tongue around the syllables of a Latin epigram? "Yeah," I hear you saying, "but it would feel a whole lot better if we knew just what the heck we were talking about." My point exactly. The world would be a much finer place if you folks knew what you were talking about. So, for those of you who may be a little rusty in the Dead Language Department, allow me to translate: "There's no accounting for taste." In other words, I don't give you grief over that horrible orange marmalade gunk you slather all over your toast, and you don't get all righteously indignant over my choice of movies. If you find your bile rising during this exegesis of Quentin Tarantino's "Pulp Fiction," take a deep breath and say to yourself: "De gustibus non est disputandum."

"Pulp Fiction" is a crude, cruel and violent movie, filled with crude, cruel and violent people. It is also very funny, and for those who can get past a few splattered brains and a boatload of bad words that we religious types aren't even supposed to know, it raises profound questions about sin and redemption, about the nature of God and the possibility of grace in a fallen world.

The "you shall love your enemies and pray for those who persecute you" incident: Butch, the slightly punch-drunk boxer played by Bruce Willis, has found himself in a world of trouble for not taking a dive in the fifth round of a fight. His boss, a gangster named Marcellus, has ordered a hit on him. The two of them run into each other and tumble into a seedy pawnshop, where they are taken captive by the proprietors, a couple of white-trash sick puppies, who proceed to torture them. Butch manages to escape and heads for freedom. But, with his hand on the door to the outside, Butch stops. There is no earthly reason for him to hesitate, no good reason to go back. Marcellus has tried to kill him, after all. The man is his enemy, but his enemy is still a man. And, for Butch, the sound of a man being tortured is the sound of the tolling bell, the one which we need never ask for whom it tolls. Butch rescues his enemy and makes, if not a friend, then at least some sort of peace with which to begin a new life.

The "blessed are your eyes, for they see" ambiguity of miracle situation: Nearly everybody in "Pulp Fiction" is looking for a new life of one kind or another. A few find it. Jules and Vince are two of Marcellus' hit men. One day, they are surprised by a gunman who jumps out of a bathroom and fires, point-blank, four, five, six, shots at them. And misses. Vince sees it as nothing more than a stroke of good luck. But Jules sees it as bona-fide miracle with life-shattering consequences: "It could be God stopped the bullets, he changed Coke into Pepsi, he found my (expletive) car keys. You don't judge (expletive) like this based on merit. Whether or not what we experienced was a . . . miracle is insignificant. What is significant is I felt God's touch. God got involved." Jules pledges to become a shepherd of lost and weak souls.

Two people witnessed the same thing: One saw luck and the other saw God. Some folks watched with their own eyes as Jesus raised the dead, and still they didn't see the hand of God. Some folks see the universe as a fluke. It all depends on how you look at it.

The redemption of the murderer Jules does not change his vocabulary; it changes his soul. Looks like God will redeem any bleepin' body. I guess there's no accounting for taste.

Christ stinks in theology of smell

ACCORDING TO THE SCIENTISTS WHO STUDY THIS SORT OF THING, the foulest-smelling substance on the face of the earth (apart from my cousin Spike) is either ethyl mercaptan or butyl seleno-mercaptan. A snootful of either of these babies would make a truckload of skunks go, "Whoa, mama! What was that?" Both of these synthetic substances (proof once again of "Better Living Through Chemistry") share the fragrant bouquet of rotting cabbage, garlic, onions, burned toast and sewer gas. Which, coincidentally, happens to be my mother's recipe for mulligan stew.

In a way, you have to feel sorry for the folks who devote their lives to this sort of thing. They had dreams, like everybody else. Dreams born in the basement with the Li'l Scientist Chemistry Set their parents gave them for their birthdays, dreams that saw them through countless dateless Friday nights, dreams that urged them on in lonely midnight lab sessions: dreams of fame, of honor, of making a difference, of (dare they even hope it?) that trip to Stockholm to pick up the Nobel Prize. And now? Now they spend their days, nostrils hip-deep in offal, rating odors on the Gag-O-Meter.

Actually, I think these olfactory researchers ought to hold their heads high (at least so they can get a shot of fresh air once in a while): The science of smell is serious business. Let's not take for granted the great strides made in the halitosis, body odor and stinky feet departments. Plus that whole scratch 'n' sniff phenomenon. It is true that for us Homo-sapiens types, the old schnoz ain't what it used to be. The Darwinian crapshoot of natural selection gave us 20/20 vision at the cost of being able to sniff out the car keys at 200 yards. That's why it takes two people these days to tell if the milk's off: "Honey, smell this for me, will you? Is this milk bad, or what?" Nonetheless, there is a powerful connection between smell and memory (one whiff of chalk dust and you're back in Mrs. Farley's fourth-grade class, conjugating verbs); smell and sex ("That's a haunting scent you're wearing. I must have you." "That's my perfume, Eau de Sweat Glands of an Agitated Civet. I'm yours."); as well as smell and health ("Sweet Mary and Joseph! What died in here?"). More than enough research to keep the guys and gals in the white lab coats hustling after grant money for years to come.

There is, moreover, a theology of smell, and here it is: Christ stinks.

It says so right in the Bible: "For we are a fragrance of Christ to God among those who are being saved and among those who are perishing; to the one an aroma from death to death, to the other an aroma from life to life" (2 Corinthians 2:15-16). Oh sure, the Apostle tries to gussy it up a bit with words like fragrance and aroma, but Paul isn't fooling anyone. The aroma of death is a stench in anybody's book. Jesus stunk. A Nazarene peasant with dirt under his fingernails, he hung around with a singularly smelly class of people: fishermen, their tunics redolent with fish guts and chum; prostitutes smelling of cheap perfume and Lord knows what else; lepers with their flesh rotting on their bones; and tax collectors (probably the worst of the lot) smelling the way tax collectors always smell. The smell of Christ is the smell of the cross: rough wood, blood, vinegar and cheap wine; the smell of fear and dying, of a world's sin. It is, at last, the smell of every sin-soaked one of us. Which is why so many of us like to keep Jesus at arm's length. We don't like to be reminded that our poop smells, that we stink to the high heavens. But it's a good thing we do, because this way, God can find us in the dark.

We need to remember, too, that from dark, thick, pungent manure comes the red, red rose. Paul says that the stink of Christ is ultimately the sweet smell of glory, of forgiveness, of love, of heaven itself. Some of us get downwind of Jesus and hold our noses; others catch a whiff and are born all over again).

Pride and the devil in shadows

THE SHADOW OF THE CHURCH WHERE I WORK falls sometimes across my backyard. The house of God throws a hard line of darkness down on my little piece of ground, and the devil lives there in the shadows. He leaves the dead people in the church cemetery alone: They've got nothing he wants. The dead rot and the dead wait and the devil calls to me and tells me I'm better than they are. Because I'm alive.

I try to live my life at high noon when all the shadows disappear, but that's not always possible. I've got things to do, heaven's work. Border crossings are inevitable, and listening to the devil in my backyard is the cost of doing business. But I'll be damned if now and again he doesn't seem to make a whole lot of sense.

Especially when the losers show up at my back door, needing food for their hungry children, or a roof over their heads for a night or two. They tell me their sad stories. Or they try to, anyway. Frankly, I'm not that interested. I've heard it before. I usually cut them off: "Let's just get to it. What is it you want from me?" And I stand on the top step at my back door so they literally have to look up to me to say what it is they're after.

The voice in the shadows reminds me I'm better than they are. I'm not the one who's screwed up his life with liquor or drugs or persistent stupidity. I'm not the one who figures he'll hit up the church for a few bucks because Christ is a soft touch.

After they tell me, and I get some feeble confirmation they are in need, I help them out. That's my job, you know: feeding the hungry, clothing the naked and all the rest of that junk. But I'll give them a hard time. I'll wonder aloud, for instance, why their own church hasn't helped them just so I can hear them tell me they don't have a church. I'll let them know they aren't fooling anybody. I'll try to shame the shameless.

Because I'm better than they are.

Last week, one of my "regulars" showed up for the second time in a month. The first time this month, he needed a room for a few nights. I gave it to him. Then he stood at the bottom of my steps asking me to lend him money for a pair of steel-toed work boots. I laughed at him and said I'd buy him a pair if he tells me where he works so I can verify the story. He wouldn't tell me, claiming that if his new boss knew he was down and out, the company would fire him.

"No name, no boots," I said, enjoying it.

He sputtered. He whined. I stood above him, proud and sure of myself.

Me and the voice in the shadows were having a high old time, when I heard my 14-year-old son at my back.

"Dad! Stop it! Give the man these boots!" Josh handed me his own steel-toed boots.

Without a word, I took them from my son and handed them to the man.

"You thank your boy for me," the man said as he left my backyard and left me in the shadows.

Josh has enough Jesus in him sometimes to scare the devil away, to change a proud and haughty father into a man who prays the poor man's prayer: "Lord have mercy on me, a sinner."

I thank God every day for my sweet boy who one day soon will be a fine and decent man.

The spiritual joy of sex

I KNOW WHAT YOU'RE DOING RIGHT NOW.

You're not having sex.

I'm right, aren't I? I really nailed that one, didn't I?

According to the results of a recently published study in the Journal of the American Medical Association, a whole lot of you are not having sex. In fact, it looks like you're making a habit of not having sex. And many of you don't even miss it.

This has to stop.

In fact, why don't you take a few minutes right now and share a little connubial bliss with your husband or wife? I'll wait right here until you finish. Just leave the paper on the coffee table. Certain portions of the anatomy look really weird covered in newsprint. (And remember, I'm only talking to you married folks out there. You fornicators are on your own, so to speak.)

Hey, you're back. Feel a whole lot better now, don't you? What's that you say? You didn't finish? It was too early in the morning, the 6-year-old burst in so you could help tie his shoes and, besides, you couldn't remember where you left the birth-control devices?

Oh, for the love of . . . work with me here, people!

You don't think I know how tough it is for you guys? Sue and I have, between us, three jobs and four kids between the ages of 2 and 16. Five kids, if you count the French exchange student who seems to be living with us these days. (Note to self: I really have to start attending those family meetings Sue schedules.)

But despite our harried lives, and the tumult in our home, Sue and I manage to make love every . . . OK, I see your point.

But this is not a good thing.

Sex is one of those marvelous gifts that a gracious God has given to humanity. When a man and woman take to the marriage bed, it is more than mere animals rutting. (Although, truth to tell, there is an element of that, and can I get an "Amen" for that?)

It is no coincidence that one of the Old Testament euphemisms for intercourse is the Hebrew verb "to know": "Now, Adam knew Eve, and she conceived and bore Cain . . ." (Genesis 4:1). Sex is knowledge, a kind of intimate knowledge of the beloved that can only be gained through touch and taste, through the touch of the lover and the sound of a wordless sigh. Naked bodies, vulnerable as they are, reveal the very soul sometimes.

Jesus was a big supporter of marital sex: "For this reason, a man shall leave his father and mother and cleave unto his wife, and the two shall be one flesh." (Mark 10:7-8) Cleaving, for all its messiness and noisiness, seems to be part of what we were made for.

God himself is revealed in the shudder and thunder of lovemaking. Sex itself can be a kind of prayer, answered in the very moment of release.

But not for a lot of you out there.

"Oh, no," you say. "We're too busy. We're too tired. We're not in the mood. We don't feel like it."

This isn't third-grade homework we're talking about here; it's fun and holy and heaven-sent.

I'll be the first to admit that even married sex can be tainted by sin, by the tendency to treat another person as an object. I'll even concede that sex all by itself is a poor substitute for true love. And nearly every Jerry Springer show ever aired does tends to prove that some people should never, ever attempt to reproduce.

But, come on.

It's a hard world out there, full of rough edges and hurt. We need to treasure every moment we get in the arms of our beloved, every naked kiss and gentle caress. That reminder, that heaven itself is within our reach, may see us and our beloved through the darkness.

The nursery school is in pageant mode

THE SHEPHERDS' ROBES ARE NO PROBLEM. I know they're looking pretty faded and ratty this year, but that's actually an advantage when it comes to outfitting children for the part of your basic dirt-poor, first-century agricultural workers. The rattier the better, I always say. Lends an air of authenticity to the proceedings. But the angels' wings are a whole other story.

The angels' wings look like they've been through hell, and when you consider that they've been worn by five or six years' worth of nursery school kids, maybe they have.

Four-year-olds can be tough on wings, take my word for it. And nothing looks worse on angels than bent wings. You can only patch and paste for so long before the heavenly hosts start dropping like flies, so I guess the nursery school teachers are going to have to make new wings for their students this year. God knows, that's going to be the least of their worries.

I can tell that Christmas is coming. The church I serve runs a nursery school, and the teachers there are in full Christmas-pageant mode. It's not a pretty sight, watching these good Christian women go rubber-room nuts, descending into some sort of maniacal funk complete with severe facial tics and a tendency to laugh out loud at inappropriate moments.

In years past, my involvement in this fandango was strictly peripheral, which was fine by me. But this year, my wife began teaching at the nursery school. I'm stuck. I'm trapped. I'm doomed. And if Jesus isn't born pretty quickly, heads are gonna roll.

You might wonder what the problem is here. You take a bunch of 4-year-olds, have them sing a couple of Christmas carols, and walk them through the Gospel Nativity scene. All the parents smile, and everybody goes home. What's the big hairy deal? Just ask Susan. On second thought, don't ask her. You haven't got that kind of time, and you'd probably like to keep your nose right there in the middle of your face.

Bringing the birth of Jesus to the stage is fraught with difficulty. In addition to making sure your angels are aerodynamically sound, you've got casting decisions to make. The Virgin Mary, for instance, cannot be prone to the giggles. This year Mary and Joseph are being played by an interracial couple, which is a nice touch. The part of Jesus will, as always, be played by a Betsy-Wetsy doll.

You've got line readings to fret over: The innkeeper does not say: "Go away. We're full! Nyahh, nyahh, nyahh!" The second of the Three Magi does not present the newborn King of Kings with a gift of Frankenstein.

You've got to hope the shepherds do not turn their staffs into nunchuckas and start whacking the farm animals upside the head. You've got to figure out which kid is going to burst into tears the minute the pageant starts and put him up front where his mom can get him easily. (I've suggested the teachers could have a lot of fun taking bets on who cries and when, but they tend to be touchy on the subject.)

No matter what happens, there is magic. One pageant, a few years ago, stays with me because of the last wise man. Each of the Magi approach the manger (you can tell the Magi because their robes are a little less ratty than the shepherds') and lay their gifts down.

"I bring gold," says the first one, in a voice full of wonder. "I bring frankincense," says the second, proud of his choice. The last wise man swaggers up to the manger, looks out at the audience and booms, "I'M BRINGIN' DA MYRRH!"

He was priceless. The wise man as wise guy. A 4-year-old gangster, all Cagney and Bogart, brought the house down. Myrrh may be a perfume, but it's also a burial spice, used to keep the dead from stinkin' up the joint. There's a poignancy to the gift in the Gospels, a gentle reminder that the Child grows up to die for us. And this little boy lets us know that if Jesus don't watch it, he'll be sleepin' with da fishes. He brought us the truth, and blessed us, and I am grateful to him.

I got into an argument at the mall the other day with a guy who claimed I stole his parking spot. Now, it was my spot free and clear, but I looked this man in the eye and said, "I'm going to let you have this spot because it is the season of peace on Earth and good will toward men." I must have touched his soul, because as he walked to his car, he suggested I perform an act that truly would take a miracle from God to accomplish.

"Oh, yeah?" I called to him, as he got in his car. "Well, I'M BRINGIN' DA MYRRH!"

Yep. Christmas is coming. I can hardly wait.

The Rileys spruce up before dinner at the Four Seasons.

Left: *Putting the finishing touches on Alex.*

Below: *From left, Joshua, Christopher, Alex and Mike getting ready to enter the restaurant.*

Above: Sam Riley, hoping for french fries, and Alex in keen anticipation.

Right: Alex looks over the menu.

Left: *Josh waits for his entree, while Sam fidgets on his dad's lap.*

Below: *Sam Riley hasn't mastered the art of sniffing the cork.*

Left: *Sharing a laugh with Captain Remo aboard the Rhapsody of the Seas.*

Below: *Mike nearly loses his balance on a rock bridge on Aruba.*

Mike contemplates the briny deep.

Left: *The nude beach at St. Martin: A Garden of Eden or Sodom and Gomorrah? A journalist investigates.*

Below: *Floundering, Mike gives up snorkeling and heads back to the boat for free rum.*

Not exactly Venus rising from the foamy sea on a clam shell.

Big Adventures

The life of Riley

In which the Riley family goes to dinner and gains an appreciation for the much-maligned barbarians

FOR REASONS AS OBSCURE AND BYZANTINE AS THE MIND OF GOD, I was recently given an unusual assignment here at the newspaper.

"Wouldn't it be a great idea," said someone in the halls of power, "to send Riley and his family to a world-class restaurant in Manhattan and have him report back on the experience?"

So, on a Saturday evening not long ago, Susan and I took our four sons to the Four Seasons Restaurant on East 52nd Street in New York City. There was Joshua, 16, the epitome of adolescent elan; Christopher, 14, our strange child, a wild card in the deck of life; Alexander, 10, funny, honest and a connoisseur of the funny noises the human body can make; and Sam, 2, who isn't quite sure how the world works but is absolutely convinced it exists solely for his benefit and pleasure.

We went. We ate. We endured.

The briefing
Or how I tried to teach my kids the rudiments of class warfare

I sat down with my children and tried to explain the situation to them. My face was grim, and they stared into my hardened eyes with trepidation.

"You know," I began, "sometimes Daddy's boss makes him do things he doesn't want to do. He's asked me, nay, ordered me to bring you all to a really fancy restaurant and spend a lot of money for supper so that I can write about it. You will have the best meal of your young lives, but you are not to enjoy it at all. We are members of the proletariat, the working class. Do you understand?"

They didn't understand.

Christopher and Alex were thrilled, out-of-their-minds delirious at the prospect of dining in the lap of luxury.

"Your boss is cool," said Christopher.

Alex did a little dance and yelled with delight. Even Sam seemed thrilled.

Only Joshua was subdued. He looked at me carefully, thoughtfully, with a wisdom beyond his years. He cleared his throat.

"Dad," he asked, "as a member of the proletariat, am I going to be allowed to order the lobster?"

The preparation
In which it is decided who is going to carry a thousand dollars
in cash through the mean streets of the big city

A week or so before our reservation, a bigwig from the newspaper asked me how I was going to pay for the impending feast.

"Do you have enough on one of your credit cards to cover the cost of this?" he asked.

Oh, how we laughed at that one.

We laughed and laughed.

By the Friday before our dinner, the company had coughed up a thousand smackers for me to buy dinner.

Susan suggested she and I divvy up the money. That way, as she put it, "If one of us gets dragged into an alley somewhere, robbed, beaten and left for dead, the rest of us will still be able to get something to eat." Practical woman, my wife.

The assault on high culture
Or a bad omen from the hatcheck girls

The Riley clan arrived at the Four Seasons a half-hour early. We'd spent the afternoon sightseeing, so the kids needed some time to make themselves presentable. They sat on steps around the corner from the front entrance to the Four Seasons and changed out of their sneakers, put on their jackets and ties and combed their hair.

Now, I realize we must have looked like we'd tumbled out of one of those tiny clown cars from the circus: six Rileys, sundry overcoats, four backpacks and a baby stroller. But I certainly didn't expect the hatcheck girls to roll their eyes at us in irritation when we checked our stuff.

But they did, and they seemed mightily vexed that they had to open a separate cloak room for our stuff, as if our stuff might be a bad influence on the other coats. I thought to myself: "Come on! You're hatcheck girls, for God's sake. Stow our belongings, and lighten up, already."

This did not bode well, I thought, as we were led down a hallway to the fabulous Pool Room, so named because there is a reflecting pool in the middle of the room.

At the table
Or what's the deal with the metal dishes?

The Rileys were seated at a round table near a window far from the kitchen. A quiet elegance, or "weirdness," as Chris put it, surrounded us.

The first thing my kids noticed were the huge metal plates on the table.

"What are they for?" asked Alex.

"I don't know," I said. Now, there's a phrase I would use a lot in the next 3-1/2 hours of this Bataan Death March of a meal.

Sam figured out what they were for. The plates were for picking up and banging on your head. He sat next to his mother in his own adult chair. There wasn't a high chair in sight, and none was offered. "Oh, so this is how it's going to be, is it? No quarter asked and none given," I thought to myself. Frankly, we were too intimidated by our surroundings to ask for a booster seat.

The Rileys frequently attend the sort of dining establishment that includes a small box of crayons, which my children use to draw on the paper place mats while waiting for the hot dogs. Not surprisingly, the Four Seasons had neither crayons nor paper place mats. All I had to offer Sam was a ballpoint pen and a small piece of paper from my reporter's notebook, which could not contain the scope of his artistic vision, so at least one tablecloth at the Four Seasons now has half a picture of Big Bird on it.

The head waiter came to our table surrounded by a small cadre of waiters and handed us our menus. The games began.

Notes on a fancy dinner

Which are mostly from memory, because the place was dark, and YOU just try to do some serious journalism when your 2-year-old is challenging your 10-year-old to a bread fight.

To tell the truth, I thought quail was a much bigger bird. Apparently, it's the ornithological equivalent of a Japanese bonsai tree. Both Christopher and Alex ordered quail as a hot appetizer. Christopher wanted to know why we didn't have this at home. Alex, believing quail is from the fried-chicken food group, picked up the tiny drumstick with his fingers and ate it that way.

I had the Beluga caviar for an appetizer (or "the $90 caviar," as Joshua prefers to call it). I slathered it on my toast points and took a bite.

"How is it, Dad?" Josh asked.

"It's a mite salty, son," I replied.

Sam's not much of a gourmet. He's more of a hard-roll kind of guy.

"Too hard," he said, as he dunked the roll repeatedly in his water glass.

The waiters were a little too efficient. Unaware that Sam uses the "Tip 'n' Sip" method of drinking, they topped off his glass only to have it spill again. And again and again in a never-ending cycle.

Of course, whenever there was not a waiter in sight, he'd raise his hand and call out, "Oh, guy. Oh, guy." Finally, Sue told him to call the man "Sir." Sam promptly knighted the staff: "Sir Guy, Sir Guy, Sir Guy."

Ninety-dollar appetizers, $17 salads ("You know how much this cost to make, Dad? Maybe a buck," Josh said.), $46 hunks of beef and arthropods, a $75 bottle of Pinot Noir ... we ordered with abandon and ate with gusto.

Well, most of us ate with gusto. Alex didn't much care for the lobster.

It was the sauce, Alex said. The product of a lifetime of culinary artistry, and my 10-year-old is acting like it's toxic waste. We had to wipe the sauce off the lobster before he'd even taste it.

On the whole, it was an exhausting meal. Sam kept fidgeting and singing "O Happy Day" at the top of his lungs. Josh was playing with his lobster claw, waving it up and down like a puppet. Chris couldn't finish his aged beef.

We all took turns taking Sam for a walk between courses ... to clear our heads, if not our palates.

By the time we ordered dessert and coffee, things had calmed down a bit. My Bananas Napoleon was quite tasty, even if it did take me a little while to actually find the banana.

Christopher and Alex got a dessert not on the menu, and as near as I could figure, absolutely free. The waiters brought them each a huge plate of white spun sugar ... cotton candy.

I'm sorry to report that before we left, Joshua started showing signs of incipient snootiness. He ordered a cappuccino with a mint "flavor shot." The waiter came by, sat the coffee down and proceeded to pour part of a vial of green liquid into the cup. The waiter walked away. Josh stared at his coffee.

"I think Sir Guy put too much mint in this," he said.

Josh took a sip.

"I knew it," he said, throwing his hand up in disgust. "This tastes like mouthwash. I can't drink this."

Maybe it was time to leave.

But not before I asked for a doggy bag for Christopher's steak. There was no way I was going to leave a $50 hunk of meat behind.

Mistakes were made
Or how I inadvertently brought the well-oiled machine, which is the Four Seasons, to a grinding halt.

Well, I forgot to smell the cork or look at the cork or lick the cork or whatever the heck it is you're supposed to do with the darned cork these days when the waiter opens the wine for you. I think I did the tasting part all right. Although my moment of sophistication was spoiled when Alex looked at the mouthful of wine in the glass and said, "Gee, Dad, is that all you get for 75 bucks?"

But that was a minor mistake.

My major gaffe at the restaurant was when I mistakenly ordered two entrees. Usually, when I go to a restaurant, the menu lists everything you get: "Philly Cheese Steak with Creamy Coleslaw and Golden Browned French Fries."

The menu at the Four Seasons wasn't like that. Nowhere did it say my steak would come with four green beans and a smidgen of mashed potatoes. So I ordered the Vegetable Platter, believing that perhaps, when it came to veggies, the Four Seasons was like a Chinese restaurant. Everybody shares.

Turns out that the vegetable platter was an entree, which threw the waiters into an absolute tizzy.

"How could such a thing happen?" they muttered. "Where, oh where, will we put the extra plate?"

Eventually, cooler heads prevailed, and they placed the plate next to my steak.

Bathroom banter
Or how I came to love "Jorge."

The bathroom at the Four Seasons is an oasis of civility, and I sought solace there many times. The first time was about 45 minutes into our ordeal. Alex and I entered a serene world of gleaming chrome and comforting marble. The men's room attendant ... let's call him "Jorge" ... quickly became my new best friend. As Alex washed his hands, a Band Aid fell off his finger. As if by magic, Jorge was by my side with a bandage in his hand. I nearly wept with joy.

He looked at me with kindness.

"Hey, boss," he said. "Maybe you'd better check your tie."

My tie was askew, my hair a mess. I had a wild-ferret look in my eyes. I composed myself under the beneficent gaze of Jorge. I loved the man and expressed that love the only way that is fitting and proper for a man to do in the men's room: I slipped him a $5 bill.

All through the night, when the pressures of dining out grew too much, one of my boys would ask me, "Can I have a dollar for the bathroom man?" I understood immediately and always obliged.

Headwaiter as deity
Or how I witnessed an epic battle for the soul of man.

Our headwaiter was tall, poised and full of self-confidence. Almost patrician. He was, in short, everything I wasn't that night. At the beginning of the evening I could tell he had sized up our little tribe pretty well. He knew we didn't belong there, and years of training allowed only a touch of condescension in his voice when he addressed us.

He fought hard against that.

At one point, he came up to me and said, "Why don't I take Sam for a little walk so you can enjoy your meal a little."

He took my baby boy in his arms and gave him a tour of the kitchen and came back 10 minutes later.

"I think your boy has a future as a chef," he said, placing him back in his chair.

It was as close to an authentic religious experience as I've ever had. The forces of darkness and snootiness had been routed by virtue and mercy.

Settling up and heading home
Or what's 20 percent of way too much money?

One thousand dollars wasn't enough. Our total bill, including tax and tip, came to $1,040. That kind of money would feed our family for six weeks. The tip alone would have paid our grocery bill for a week. We tipped the headwaiter, our savior, big time.

"Thank you," I said to him.

"Listen," he said to me. "Don't worry. It was my pleasure."

As Susan and I gathered the clan together, a woman at the table next to us said: "I have to commend you. Your sons are wonderfully behaved, and you should be proud of them. My little boy is 2, and I wish I had brought him here tonight."

"No, you don't, lady. No, you don't," I said. "This is no place for a 2-year old."

Depending on who you listen to, food is love or sex or art. Maybe so. Right now, all I know is, eating it can be damned hard work in a world-class restaurant.

Reunited 1976-1996

And it feels so good. Michael Riley, West Deptford High School Class of 1976, recently attended his 20th reunion.

"Twenty years now, where'd they go? Twenty years, I don't know."
"Like A Rock," Bob Seger

"Lucy, you know the world must be flat 'cause when people leave town, they never come back."
"Small Town Saturday Night," Hal Ketchum

I WENT TO MY 20-YEAR HIGH SCHOOL REUNION LOOKING FOR JUSTICE. I wanted to see broken-down athletes, cheerleaders gone fat and frumpy, bullies and jerks humbled and bitter. But on this Friday night, the athletes all looked tanned and fit, moving with grace and smoking fat cigars. The cheerleaders were still gorgeous. And the knuckle-draggers were unfailingly polite and walking upright.

Maybe there is no justice in this world.

On the other hand, I got to slow dance with Jody Williams, proving once again that justice is highly over-rated.

The West Deptford High School Class of 1976 reunion was a swell affair – surprisingly swell, considering that our class was not particularly known for putting on swell affairs. The Homecoming theme our senior year was "Stairway to Heaven," that Led Zeppelin ode to mysticism or hallucinogens or something. The best minds in the class came up with the Homecoming float: a stepladder wrapped in aluminum foil. So my expectations were not that high.

Adding to my anxiety was the fact that the place chosen for the reunion was Auletto Caterers ballroom, the very site of our senior prom. (Theme: "April Showers Bring May Flowers." I think the float involved a garden hose and a package of Burpee seeds.)

Now, in high school, I dated precisely two women. The first was a generous, funny, loving girl whom my parents forbade me to see because of the color of her skin. Donna and I sneaked around for a while, but the pressure was too much for us, and we broke up. On the rebound, I hooked up with a girl two years younger, a truly horrible human being who had me convinced, for the three years that we were together, that she was about as good as a wretch like me could ever expect in the way of female companionship.

It was this harpy I took to the prom, even though we were in the midst of one of those pitched battles that characterized the dirty little war that was our relationship. Not that I'm bitter or anything. But there were ghosts around me as I walked into that ballroom.

I went to the reunion alone. My wife, Sue, summed up her position this way: "Why would I want to sit around for hours talking to people I don't know, discussing times I never had?" I reminded her that Dear Abby and Ann Landers are always printing letters from women who sent their husbands off to high-school reunions alone only to find that the guy takes off for a roll in the hay with a 40-year-old divorcee and a new life in Tahiti.

"I'll take my chances," Sue said.

There were plenty of spouses in attendance, most there as part of a quid-pro-quo arrangement: "I went to his (hers), so you bet he (she) was coming to mine." They were all very patient, these spouses, smiling and trying to get into the spirit of the thing. My friend Gary Biester brought his new bride, Ianna, and promptly left her at our table to go reminiscing. "Gary's going to pay for this, you know," she said, with what can only be called an evil smile. "Not in the car on the way home and not all at once. This is good for six, eight months of revenge." I told Gary I really liked his bride.

Some spouses really didn't have a choice. Tim and Debbie, for instance. Voted "Cutest Couple" in 1976, they were still cute as the dickens and still a couple 20 years later. Tim was late because their two sons were playing in the Big Game that night, just as their father had done so many years before. In fact, the West Deptford High football team is coached these days by Don Clark, the guy who for four years had the locker right next to mine and who spent most of his high school career trying to prove that I could, in fact, fit inside my locker.

He greeted me warmly that night, despite the fact that his Eagles had lost the Big Game. And apart from a bone-crushing handshake ("Hand Mangling 101": a required three-credit course in gym teacher school, I'm sure), he acted like a regular human being.

There was something gentle and life-affirming in the fact that so many folks at the reunion had stayed put, making families and dreams in the same place they swore in the yearbook they would get as far away from as possible. Which is not to say that everybody stuck around. Gary Gotchell moved to Germany for love, returning to his wife's homeland after a few years in the States. It was Gotchell who, a few hours into the festivities and, with perhaps a bit of schnapps in him, responded to my statement that I was a minister and a journalist by shouting "You've got to pick, Riley! You can't be both! You've got to choose!"

If your life's really bad, you wouldn't be here

The reunion couldn't really get under way without announcements from Patty S., whom I remembered as an interminably perky student council something or other. She would open our assemblies with a voice that could sterilize livestock at 75 yards. She's now an interminably perky tenured professor at a New England college whose amplified voice could still probably drop a bull moose in its tracks. She gave out prizes at the reunion for those who'd come the farthest (which I missed by approximately 10,000 miles) and for the alumnus with the most children (which I missed by one, but I'll be damned if I'm going to have a fifth kid just to win a pair of plastic maracas).

There was plenty of dinner conversation at the reunion. We talked about the teachers we remembered. Not the best teachers, not the ones who had made an impact on our lives. We talked about the gym teacher who dated the cheerleader, the science teacher who would periodically sign himself into an asylum for a few weeks of "quiet time." And we talked about Mr. Koschreck, an English teacher who once dropped my grade to an A- in sophomore Composition because I used the word "psyche" in an essay. "No 15-year-old can possibly know what the word psyche means," he told me. Mr. Koschreck was my favorite teacher until one day in our junior year when he went home, got a shotgun and killed his wife, his 5-year-old daughter and his dog before turning the gun on himself and blowing his own psyche all over the living room wall.

Dead teachers are one thing. Dead classmates are a whole other thing. The last page of our souvenir booklet pictured those of our class who had passed away. Frozen in time, they smiled at us from 20 years ago, full of hope and promise. But AIDS claimed one, cancer stole a few more, hopelessness killed one by his own hand, accidents the rest.

I could only bear witness for one of them. I had reconnected with the valedictorian of our class, Susan Gonia, after our 10th class reunion. Bored with every job she had ever had, one bad marriage behind her, she was on her way to California to begin a new career as a triathlete when she was struck and killed by a car. Her mother wrote me a nice note, thanking me for being her friend. But there are some who will not go down without a fight. Dawn S. was at the reunion, fighting and winning a harrowing battle with bone-marrow cancer. "I had a lot to be thankful for this Thanksgiving," she told me.

Sex, drugs, rock 'n' roll: Two down, one to go

Most of us haven't smoked dope in years. Rock 'n' roll has moved from the central passion of our lives to mere background music. Which leaves sex.

I fell into more conversations about the female orgasm than is healthy for a Baptist minister. Hell, in high school, I didn't even know females had orgasms. Twenty years later, they have 'em, are empowered by 'em and talk about 'em in front of everybody. I know that doctors at parties get asked about lumbago and tennis elbow. As a minister, I always get the "sex in heaven" question: "Doesn't heaven feel like one big orgasm?" I usually answer: "I'll have to get back to you on that." Then I head for the bar.

At the bar the night of the reunion I ran into Paul, a truly nice guy who seems to be wrapping up the first half of his life in the position that nice guys usually wind up in. He told me that he was happy, had a good job and had never married. "Women usually just want to be friends with me," he said. This sounded eerily like conversations I'd had with him over mystery meat and green beans in the school cafeteria, so I headed back to my table.

Just in time for the disc jockey to get started. Now a lot of great music came out of the '70s: The Stones and The Who still rocked. Roots rockers like Seger, Springsteen and Mellencamp were catching on. But for this DJ, the mid-'70s meant one thing: disco. For a change of pace he played the "Macarena." I went back to the bar. "You know," I said to a group of guys at the rail, "the appearance and persistence of this dance is a sure sign that the apocalypse is nigh."

"Nothing ever changes, Riley," said Andy C. "Twenty years later and here we are at a dance, standing in the back, making fun of the people who actually dance."

He had a point. Yet, the purpose of a reunion is to make a connection to who we were and who we are. People came up to me throughout the night, telling me how funny I'd been in school, how profound, how brave I was, skirting the edge of danger by making fun of big, lumbering classmates in ways just shy of getting my backside kicked. And I kept thinking all night long, "Where the hell were these people 20 years ago, when I was a cliqueless cipher in high school and could have used a little ego stroking?"

Abelard and Heloise at the sock hop

I knew where Jody Williams was 20 years ago. Two rows over in American History I and in my dreams and my fantasies. She was the kind of girl Raymond Chandler wrote about: "A blonde to make a bishop kick a hole in a stained-glass window." She was also the type for whom the phrase "out of my league" was invented.

One day she discovered that I was an atheist and, gripped with fear for my soul, wrote me a letter. I wrote back. Tongue-tied and clumsy, although in league with the devil, I could write up a storm. I went to church just to keep her writing and the rest is history: I saw the light, found Jesus, became a minister.

I don't think she ever knew how I hungered for her. Until this reunion. She walked in wearing red and looking like her presence would have archbishops and cardinals ready to kick the old stained glass. I confessed to her. To my surprise she told me she'd kept my letters for years, that she'd thought about me often.

In an unorthodox rendering of Christian theology, she told me: "I always figured that God would cut me some slack for getting you and him together." It turns out she's a divorced nurse with a girl and a boy. She asked me to dance and the years flew away. "You know, Mike," she said, "this life is not one I would have ever imagined for myself. It's hard sometimes. But it's a good life, and it's mine."

At the end of the reunion, we were 20 years older if not 20 years wiser, and the Class of 1976 went off into the night to claim those lives: good ones, hard ones and ours.

Coming to grips with science

SOME THINGS YOU HAVE TO TAKE ON FAITH: the existence of a merciful God, say, or the trustworthiness of your true love. Whether or not your recent vasectomy "took" is not one of those things. What you want there is the cold, hard light of empirical science to shine. Prayer, hope and luck is fine stuff – stuff that will take you far in this world, and even farther into the next. But when it comes to making sure the miracle of conception will forever more pass me by, I'll take a nurse in a white lab coat over a heartfelt "Now I lay me down to sleep" and three four-leaf clovers any day of the week.

About two months after the birth of my fourth son, Samuel (who is still the most beautiful baby in the world), I had a vasectomy, assuming I would be infertile from the moment I hopped off the operating table. (Actually, "hopped" is not quite the right word. One does not hop anywhere in the immediate aftermath of that particular procedure. What one does is move in much the same slow, deliberate manner as Elmer Fudd when he is hunting "wabbits.") But vasectomies don't equal immediate sterility. In the first place, you've still got front-line troops with live ammo ready to make one last suicide mission. In the second place, sometimes the operation goes kerflooey, and severed things reconnect.

The scientific method confirms that all is proceeding according to plan – without either anomaly or fluke – through repeated experimentation, which is how I came to be in possession of "the cup."

At intervals of two and six weeks after my operation, I had to go back to the doctor's office with the fruits of my scientific endeavors in hand. Actually, "in hand" is not quite the most precise phrase: The cup and the aforementioned fruits were in a small, brown paper bag. My sample was whisked away to some back-room laboratory and tested for signs of life. In a matter of minutes, the results were relayed to me.

I've come away from the whole experience convinced the Lord made me screw up in high-school calculus class so I would not choose science as a career. Here's what I learned about that vaunted world:

SCIENCE IS A LONELY, NERVE-WRACKING BUSINESS.

The cup sat in my medicine chest, where it would mock me every morning. When the day came to finally put it to use, performance anxiety was at an all-time high. And with a cranky newborn and a sleep-deprived wife at home, I couldn't count on any assistance. I had to plumb the mysteries of life all by myself. A life of faith, by contrast, thrives in the community of the madding crowd.

SCIENCE CAN BE EMASCULATING.

Certain feminists claim Western religion and science are chauvinistic and patriarchal. It seems to me gravity and redemption do their work without regard to the gender of the person who falls down and goes boom. All I know is certain scientific procedures can knock your manhood for a loop. Have I mentioned the specimen cup was about the size of a 7-Eleven Big Gulp? In that context, my "science project" seemed pitifully inadequate.

Blind faith and crossed fingers have no place in the sterile empiricism of Occam's razor and Bacon's scientific method. But a strong faith must embrace science. Because science reveals God's wild and grace-filled extravagance, which fills all the teeming worlds of the Milky Way with the jots and tittles of life and matter and energy. It is science that blessedly frees me from jots or tittles of any kind. And for that I praise the Lord.

Out of my "unmade bed," out of my league

How I, a humble man of God, found myself thrust into a world of runways, champagne flowing like water, bosomy designers and a Siberian supermodel who's looking to connect with the universe

WHEN I WAS ASKED TO COVER FASHION WEEK in New York City, I was flattered.

"Ah," I said to myself, "they recognize my superior reporting skills, my keen eye for detail, my incisive use of words as vehicles for truth and beauty."

Wrong. The decisive factor in my getting this assignment was, according to reliable sources, the fact that I look (quote) like an unmade bed (unquote).

Some people are born great; others have greatness thrust upon them. I'm just rumpled.

Frankly, I wasn't sure I was up to the job. And it's not like I didn't have enough to do otherwise. But, like Jesus in the wilderness, I was tempted.

"You'll get to meet supermodels," they told me.

Jesus got out of the desert with his virtue intact.

Not me.

"I'm there," I said.

Actually, it wasn't that easy. Security is tight at 7th on Sixth. Apparently, you can't have just anybody waltzing in to look at clothes. When I went to pick up my press credentials, my name wasn't on "the list." Story of my life. Luckily, Pam Gallagher showed up to rescue me.

I hook up with my tour guide for our descent into the abyss

When Dante visited the inferno, his traveling companion was Virgil, a "good pagan" with the soul of a poet. Who do they send to accompany me on my perilous journey into decadence and good taste? Pam Gallagher, a fashion editor with a big dose of attitude.

"This is Michael Riley, an ordained minister," she tells the harried woman behind the 7th on Sixth desk at the tents. "He's with me." A quick phone call later and I'm in. Pam explains to me that the whole "meek shall inherit the earth" stuff is fine for the pulpit, but it ain't gonna cut any ice among the fashion swells. "You have to act like you belong here," she coaches me.

With a haughty wave of her hand, she gets me into places I have no business being. We move to the front row of runway shows, settling into chairs reserved for fashion writers from the New York Post. By the end of my second day in the fashion world, I'm walking past guarded velvet ropes like an old pro. Pam and I are the Bonnie and Clyde of the fashion media.

What I know now about fashion models

I actually recognized many of the women walking up and down the runways at the various Bryant Park venues. They were every girl who never talked to me in high school. They had that same blank stare, the one with a hint of silent reproof and naked disdain.

Speaking of naked, runway models think absolutely nothing of showing their breasts. (This, of course, is nothing like the behavior of every girl in high school who never spoke to me.) Except for the wedding gowns, nearly every article of clothing I saw was sheer on top, revealing small, perky, perfectly formed breasts. It was along about the time I was watching the tenth set of revealed breasts slinking past me that I realized this assignment was probably sending me to hell.

Models walk funny. They move up the runway with a sort of "I've -got -a-stiff -neck -but -I-still -want- to -win- the- limbo-contest" kind of thing. Head straight, hips thrust forward and a one-foot-in-front-of-the- other gait that makes them look like Russian gymnasts on the balance beam in high heels.

Some things you need to know if you plan to attend fashion week

1. For a multi-million dollar extravaganza of glitz, they really skimp on the necessities, if you ask me. The porta-potties they set out for the attendees were really state of the art. In fact, there was this whole...procedure...you had to go through involving foot pedals that fill the bowl with blue water. I never thought I'd need a master's degree in aerospace engineering just to relieve myself of all the free Moet & Chandon I'd been swilling. And couldn't they at least stock the joint with a couple extra rolls of double ply?

2. Watch out for the booby-trapped hors d'oeuvres. I realize that a single plate of hors d'oeuvres could feed the the entire East Coast model population for a week. What I hadn't counted on was how hard it would be to get one all the way to my mouth. We were at Grand Central Terminal for a self-congratulatory press reception hosted by the Council of Fashion Designers of America when I was approached by a waiter who was the very epitome of androgyny.

"Watercress and crabmeat?" the waiter asked. I reached down and picked one up, forgetting that watercress doesn't have the heft of, say, a Ritz cracker. I wound up with crabmeat on my shirt and danger- ously slippery watercress on the floor. A word of advice to those planning next year's shindig: You can't go wrong with pigs in a blanket.

3. Don't forget your uniform. For all the avant-garde, cutting-edge sensibility of the fashion media, everybody dresses just like everybody else. I've never seen so many black turtlenecks in my life. I half expect- ed Lenny Bruce or Mort Sahl to show up.

What are the hot new trends for spring?

Beats the hell out of me.

"Look for themes," Pam told me as we moved from show to show. I tried. Lord knows I tried. But the clothes I saw were all over the map. And the programs for the shows seemed to be written in some foreign language. What the hell is tulle, anyway? And why can't designers stick to colors like red and blue and green and yellow? Pink is a color; salmon is a fish.

Here are some of the things I saw at various fashion shows. I hope this is helpful as you, a normal-type person, go about the business of selecting your spring wardrobe:

One of the hot new colors seems to be a kind of carwash-sponge brown.

I saw a two-piece bathing suit the dark-green color of Army fatigues, sort of a "Baywatch"-hits- Omaha-Beach kind of thing.

Anna Sui wants us to believe that the '60s are coming back, with hot pants and headbands and pants that lace up the side. It looks like Laurie Partridge drops acid and joins a free-love commune. You're not gonna be able to wear these to Sunday Mass.

The Levintza collection seems to evoke a definite "Buffy the Vampire Slayer-goes -to-the- Starship

Enterprise- and-celebrates -Cinco de Mayo" ambience.

Bob Mackie expects you to look really swanky at the next PTA meeting.

On high fashion and ontological impossibility

I'm an intelligent and tolerant man. I minored in philosophy. I know a few things about paradox and mystery and ambiguity. But I have to admit, when I read about the "handless gloves," I was stumped. Even Plato would tell you that the concept of "glove" is tied inextricably to the notion of "hands." But there it was in black-and-white, right on the program for the Levintza show. In a few minutes, I was promised a look at something that should not, could not, possibly exist in a world governed by reason and the laws of physics. It turns out that a handless glove is a tube of cloth that runs from above the wrist to below the shoulders. It's more like a leg warmer for the arms than a glove.

Of course, the handless gloves fit in quite nicely with Angel Sanchez's new invention: the pocket without sides or a bottom. That's right, pants with a loop of cloth where the pockets should be. The only practical value of these pants would be for young mothers at the supermarket. The kids could reach up and grab the loops like subway straps. Except that these pants also have hip slits, which means your butt is periodically exposed to the elements. Not the perfect garb for that trek through the frozen food department.

John Bartlett assures us that his clothes have "multiple personalities." Just what we need: clothes that need Thorazine before you can take them out of the closet.

Don't get me started: The highly offensive pants of Marithe & Francois Girbaud

I didn't think it was possible for clothes to get me angry, to cause the bile to rise in my throat, but the Girbauds' show really ticked me off. It started out with some fey guy reading some obtuse poem about slashes and holes and time and space and the nature of existence. Then they come out, a dozen surly male and female adolescents. I'm thinking, "Damn! I've got two of these at home. I had to come all the way to the Big City to watch this?"

Guess what, moms and dads?

Even baggier pants are on the way. Baggy pants with HUGE pockets. Most of these ensembles include chains that run from knee to breastbone or waist to knee.

Actually, most of these clothes look like they were slapped together by a home ec class working from a Simplicity pattern, and when they weren't finished when the bell rang, they said, "Ah, the hell with it. We'll wear it like this."

There seemed to me to be a subtext of self-mutilation to the whole ugly business.

Strange, offensive clothes. But maybe that's the point.

The simple faith and outrageous hospitality of Betsy Johnson

Hard-working fashion guys like me need to unwind at the end of a long day. We need to kick back and party hearty. Designer Betsey Johnson understands that. She threw us a party. Which is how I happened to be at some hot nightclub called Lot 61 at 11 o'clock on a Tuesday night. (Don't these people have sitters to take home? Don't they have jobs to go to in the morning?) Lot 61 has the look of a refurbished warehouse and the charming decadence of '30s Berlin nightlife.

Pam and I spent most of the evening trying to scope out the turf, which is not possible without a snootful of Betsey Johnson's free booze. Once Pam assured me that, despite its name and pink color, the Cosmopolitan is not, in fact, a "girly drink," I made sure I had three or four of them. They helped me to focus on the fuzzy big-screen display of Johnson's latest creations. But mostly, the liquor allowed me to unashamedly stare at the two intoxicated lesbians sharing the chair in front of me. Which I would have done until the cows came home, except that Pam kept distracting me by pointing out the transvestites in attendance.

A few years ago, Pam said, Betsey Johnson presented a trailer trash-themed fashion show. Having grown up in a trailer park, I don't think it was very nice of Betsey to hold us up to fashion ridicule. But a few free drinks forgiveth much, as the Good Book says (or ought to say, anyway). Betsey Johnson in person looks like every middle-aged mother who ever embarrassed her daughter by trying to be cool. Boisterous, with a great shock of scarecrow hair and an abundance of cleavage, Betsey smiled brightly at me. Her daughter Lulu (no slouch in the cleavage department herself) stood, unembarrassed, next to her mom. The story I heard is that Lulu and Betsey got their breast implants together,4 putting the lie to the conservative rant that family values are nonexistent among the fashion glitterati.

I introduced myself to Betsey by telling her that I was a religion writer.

"I love God!" she shouted at me.

And God must love Betsey. According to Pam, she's been in business for at least 25 years, which is long by fashion designer standards.

They started charging for the drinks. It was time to go home. As we left, somebody handed me a Betsey Johnson goody bag. I am now the proud owner of a hot pink Betsey Johnson toothbrush. I think it was a really nice gesture, even though the words "dental hygiene" do not immediately spring to mind when one thinks of Ms. Johnson.

Irina, snowflakes, Siberian starshine and the secret of the universe

I could be in love. The Siberian supermodel Irina is tall and beautiful and a fairy-tale princess. Even if she is shilling jewelry at a party in an upscale clothing store on a Wednesday night. If I wasn't happily married to my own fairy-tale princess, I could fall for a woman like this. She takes my hand in hers and I use the old "religion writer" line.

When she speaks of theology, even if it is warmed-over Spinoza with a touch of Far Eastern inscrutability thrown in, it sounds like music. And I haven't even started drinking the Siberian Tang martinis yet, bright blue drinks that look like radioactive Kool-Aid.

"I want to be connected to every part of the universe," Irina says to me, her eyes shimmering like snowflakes falling on the Siberian steppes and afire with the answers to all life's questions. "I think the universe is very important."

It takes me two of the blue drinks to clear my head and get ready to eat dinner.

At the end of the day, it's all just clothes

Pam and I had dinner in one of the city's chic little cafes to discuss this Gomer Pyle-goes-to-Vegas adventure of mine in the white-hot vortex of fashion.

Speaking of designers, Pam said, "There are worse ways to make a living, you know."

Which is true, as far as it goes. But I can't help thinking that there may not be any more useless way to make a living because, let's face it, clothes are for covering up and keeping warm.

For me, the bottom line is this: Pants is just pants.

Join us for a five day cruise as we explore the world passengers rarely see at sea.

BELOW DECKS
A city on the waves

Dedication, elbow grease make pleasure palace shine

SATURDAY, MARCH 27, 1999. SAN JUAN, PUERTO RICO.

There is a city.

It floats in warm, azure waters, rising over 100 feet in the air under deep blue skies.

People come to live a carefree week in this floating city where humdrum tedium and worldly pressures are transferred, even temporarily, to the shoulders of those below deck.

This is the passengers' time.

Many of them saved for months or even years to pay the cost of admission. They come: infants and octogenarians, families and lovers, strangers and friends. They want to play with abandon and live like kings and queens for a brief moment. The sun on their backs, the sea breeze in their hair, they move from port to port when the floating city moves.

In San Juan on the last Saturday in March, more than 3,000 people find themselves on board Royal Caribbean's M/S Rhapsody of the Seas, bound for Aruba, Curacao, St. Martin and St. Thomas.

A million dollars in provisions as well as the means to produce 300 liters of water every day for each person on board have been stowed below decks. The millions of gallons of fuel are even now being prepared for injection in the diesel engines. A total of 1,000 guest staterooms have been cleaned since this morning when the last group of passengers left the ship to go home. Hours later the ship is ready to go.

Joining me among the passengers are my wife, Susan, photographer Joe McLaughlin and his wife, Judy. We are there to discover how the city works: Under the glittering city ... in the in-between spaces of that stately pleasure dome that is the modern cruise ship ... is another town, a place where the everyday realities of life are handled.

Aboard the Rhapsody of the Seas, there is a hospital manned by a staff of five ... two doctors and three nurses. There's a shopping mall, bakery, dry cleaners, movie theater, post office, beauty salon, video arcade, bingo parlor, dance hall, a putting green and, of course, an ATM. There's even a morgue and a two-cell jail. If you've got it in your neighborhood at home, it's on board.

Crew members, though, live in a different neighborhood from the passengers. Their world has no gleaming brass railings on the stairways, no breakfast in bed nor chocolate mints on their pillows.

Among those who are there for the sole purpose of making everything easy for the paying guests is Roger Bennett, a 34-year-old Costa Rican. He's been a cabin attendant for more than a decade. He makes up 17 rooms twice a day, working from early morning to late at night. He wonders sometimes if he's "traded his youth for wealth."

And bartender XL Sun, born in Beijing 30 years ago and looking someday to strike it rich.

And Chief Engineer Harald Hansen, who marvels over that fact that a single exercise bike in the ship's gym contains more electronics than the ships he sailed 20 years ago.

This is a polyglot city: The 777 members of the crew represent 55 nations. Many of them work 14- to 16-hour days, 7 days a week, for six months at a time. It's a hard life, yet many of them find their way back again and again.

It's a city with its own fiefdoms. The captain and bridge officers are all Norwegians. The security officer is a retired Royal Navy officer. His staff is Filipino.

It's a city on the move: The captain pilots this 915-foot long vessel weighing more than 78,000 tons with a single joystick.

It's a transient city: Nearly two-thirds of the population ... the passengers ... move out every seven days.

Both cities exist side by side on the high seas. It's the hard work of the crew that makes the magic of the floating city possible. Muscle and machines bring the food, clean the rooms, and make the cares and worries of the passengers nonexistent.

Bon voyage!

The cruise begins on a steamy night. The holiest week of the Christian year is about to begin. The dogs of war are howling at the moon half a world away in Kosovo.

Me? With NATO missiles screaming through the European night, I'm standing in a crowd at Muster Station 11 on Deck 5 of the M/S Rhapsody of the Seas getting lifeboat instructions.

There are about 125 of us gathered together for the lifeboat drill. With the big orange life jackets we're all wearing, we look like highway workers.

My wife, Susan, and I are far in the back of the crowd. We can't make out exactly how we're actually supposed to get into the lifeboat dangling above our heads. There is going to be real trouble if we hit an iceberg, we think. Nor can I hear whether or not that silly "women and children first" rule is still being enforced.

Eventually, word filters back to us that we are supposed to wait for our cabin number to be called and then yell out the number of people staying there.

It takes 20 minutes for people to stop answering "Here!" or "Ho!" or "Present!" and start shouting out numbers. A kind of giddy fatigue infects the crowd. Many of us boarded the ship today only after a long, arduous day of travel. It's time for the fun to start, but our bodies are hoping that the fun can start tomorrow. Maybe that's why few people seem to be listening to the instructions.

Or maybe, it's for the same reason nobody pays much attention to the airline safety talk at the beginning of the flight. We've heard it before or we've watched "Titanic" or we can't really believe that a ship this big could ever really run into trouble.

When we're finally dismissed, someone in the crowd yells, "Muster Station 11 rules!"

The crowd laughs and heads back inside the ship.

After the lifeboat drill, there is an introductory talk in one of the theaters. Cruise Director Laurie Rizzo attempts to whip up the rapidly flagging crowd with banter and audience participation.

"When anybody asks how you are this week, you have to pump your hand in the air and say "Excellent!' OK, let's try it," she says. It take a while to get some enthusiasm going, but she succeeds.

Not everybody went to hear the pep talk. Some folks staked out seats in the gambling hall.

The Casino Royale was scheduled to open at 11 p.m., but at 10:45 p.m. passengers were already sitting in front of slot machines with quarters in their hands.

At 11:01, a passenger yells out, "Turn on the machines." A minute later the ring and trill sounds of one-armed bandits are heard throughout the room.

Maybe some of those gamblers prayed for luck because God Himself has his place in The Floating City.

Finding "The City of God'

The irony was as thick as a wine steward's accent.

To get to the 8:30 a.m. Palm Sunday Mass, you had to walk through the ship's casino. The Casino Royale was closed but the bright lights on the quarter slots were flickering to beat the band.

Once you walked through the casino, you found a seat up front in the Broadway Melodies Lounge. The Christian clergyman on board this week is a retired 81-year-old Roman Catholic bishop from California, the Most Rev. Juan Azube. He would conduct a Mass each day on board. A Jewish cantor provided Passover and Sabbath services.

Bishop Juan, as he likes to be called, is a small man with a face almost glowing with inner peace. He stands on stage and adjusts his miter.

"I wore this this morning so you'd know I'm a bishop," he says with a smile to the 80 or so Catholics gathered in the theater. He tells the congregation a little bit about himself. Born in Ecuador, with a degree in engineering, he worked in Hollywood for a while, dubbing voices for Spanish versions of American films.

"I was Peter Lorre's voice in "The Maltese Falcon'," he says with an uncanny imitation of the late actor.

Bishop Juan begins asking for volunteers to join him on stage for a sort of Passion Play/Scripture Reading. He finds his Judas, a young man in the congregation.

"That will be your penance for today," he says.

I'm not sure that the actual apostles ever wore Bermuda shorts, but the service seems meaningful to those who've come to share the Eucharist. Accompanying Bishop Juan this week is his assistant, a former seminarian named Ron Zurawaski.

"It's a good gig," Zurawaski says. "We're sort of in between the passengers and the crew. We get a free ticket to the ship and pay our own airfare. The cruise lines usually prefer to have a Catholic priest on board because a priest can lead a Protestant worship service. This week, there's also a Jewish cantor on board to lead a Passover seder and conduct Sabbath services. It's tough to get a priest during Holy Week, though, but the bishop can do it because he's retired. I believe this his eighth cruise."

Holy Week presents its own challenges, however. The somber Good Friday liturgy, in particular, seems a bit strange when held on a pleasure cruise.

At the conclusion of the Good Friday service, Bishop Juan blesses a small group of passengers and crew.

"May you find all your loved ones safe at home," he says, and walks to the doorway of the Shall We Dance Lounge. The devout greet him as they head into the Schooner Bar. They don't often come to him for pastoral counseling during the cruise.

"People tend to leave their problems at home," Azube says.

Zurawaski gathers the music and altar supplies.

"There is a stark contrast between the opulence of our surroundings and Good Friday, a day that should be given over to fasting, prayer, and penitence," he says with a wry smile.

Before he can finish, Danielle Topping, the social hostess, walks in and begins setting up for a Trivia Game.

Topping, a native of England, has a sort of Spice Girl perkiness about her. Sometimes, she's everywhere at once: leading a dance line at the pool at night, running party games or manning the ship's library in the morning. On Palm Sunday, I watch her lead a 10-minute early-morning interdenominational worship for five sleepy Protestants. The hymns come through her boombox.

I asked her how she got stuck with this job.

"I volunteered," she says with a smile.

It's good to know that God is present on the high seas, but I still wanted to meet His co-pilot, the captain of The Rhapsody of The Seas.

BELOW DECKS
Hitting the jackpot: Cranbury pair count on a relaxing, fun time

THIS IS LINDA PENNEY'S SECOND CRUISE.

The sixth-grade math teacher at Cranbury School went the first time with her husband, Jack.

He stayed home this week to work on his golf game.

"Three's a crowd," Penney explains.

Accompanying Penney aboard the Rhapsody of the Seas this week is her 81-year-old mother, Helen Mason. It's her first cruise. You can tell because she hasn't quite mastered the art of where to put the sunblock. By midweek, the bridge of her nose is lobster-red bright.

But the sunburn has not dimmed her spirits. She's in her glory.

"I call all the shots," she says.

Her daughter smiles indulgently.

"The only thing I was permitted to do without her all week was walk on the upper deck every morning," Penney says.

Penney and Mason stay away from the more arduous shore excursions when the ship is in port. No SCUBA-diving or 8-hour jeep tours for them.

"Mom's the shopper," Penney says, and sure enough, you can see the two of them wandering through the shopping areas of the island cities, bags in hand. Some of the time, it looks like Penney has a hard time keeping up with her mother.

Other times, mother and daughter rest in the early afternoon, sitting in deck chairs poolside. They need to conserve their strength. They're unavailable for conversation between 5 and 6 p.m. every day. That's bingo time.

"Mom's the shopper," Penney says. "And the gambler."

Indeed, if you ask Mason what her favorite part of the cruise is, she says, without much enthusiasm, that "the scenery is wonderful." But push her a little, and she'll tell you the truth: The casino is her favorite place to be. "Mom closed down the casino last night," says Penney, at dinner on Friday.

Not that Penney has much to complain about. She hit a $750 jackpot on the quarter slots Wednesday night. Her picture is in a glass case at the entrance to the casino.

"I've enjoyed the cruise immensely," Mason says. "And it's because of my daughter that I was able to make it."

All good things come to an end. Saturday afternoon at the San Juan Airport, waiting for the delayed flight back to Newark, Mason is catching a catnap.

Penney finally is getting around to grading the homework papers she's been lugging around all week.

Below Decks
Facing temptation: "Friends" can meet on board

EACH NIGHT OF THE CRUISE, a four-page newsletter, the Cruise Compass, is delivered to each passenger's cabin. It lists the next day's shipboard activities, everything from the early morning "Gutbusters" abdominal workout to the late-night "Country and Western Hoe-Down."

I was reading my copy one night when I came upon this listing: "4:00 p.m.-5:00 p.m FRIENDS OF BILL W. MEETING ... Viking Crown Lounge, Deck 11, upper level."

It seemed odd to me that there would be an AA meeting (Bill W. was the founder of the organization and "Friends of Bill W." is sort of a euphemism for Alcoholics Anonymous among those who don't want to broadcast their presence) on a cruise ship, a place which sometimes seems given over to eating and drinking. Odder still that the meeting would be held in a bar on board.

I arrived at Viking Crown Lounge a little early. There were no signs in the nearly deserted bar. One by one, people walked in, looked around and waited. In a few moments, three recovering alcoholics found each other at sea, just as they find each other all over the world. They sat at a table together, ordered soft drinks and began talking to one another.

There are Jack and Katherine, a married couple from California, and John from New Jersey. Complete strangers on a vacation in paradise greeted one another like old friends, which, in a way, they were. They'd traveled the same dark roads years ago, blinded to beauty by their disease.

They all agree that they probably wouldn't have taken a cruise for the first couple of years of their recovery. The temptations might have been too much./p

"Thank God, it's different today," says Katherine. "But meetings like this help keep us grounded."

John has been on cruises before, he says, and on every one them, the Friends of Bill W. have gathered for these kind of impromptu meetings.

Jack doesn't see any incongruity between the life aboard ship where one can't travel the length of the ship without passing someplace offering booze and his presence here.

"Hey," he says, "We like to do a lot of things. We like to have fun. We just don't drink."

BELOW DECKS
Sometimes, you need a dose of reality in Paradise

LIFE ON BOARD THE RHAPSODY OF THE SEAS has an unreal serenity to it.

The passengers, pampered and coddled, are full of smiles and laughter.

And the members of the crew wear the long hours, the spartan lives and the long time at sea as a badge of honor. They smile, too ... morning, noon, and night.

"We want to make you happy," they say with feeling.

After a while, though, you begin to long for a note of contention, a pebble in the shoe, something, anything to bring you back to reality and remind you that you are not just dreaming.

It's true that the ship print shop, hidden down on Deck 0 and looking for all the world like the back room at Kinko's, makes available to passengers a fax digest of The New York Times. But a digest is hardly a newspaper and barely a reminder of the "real" world on land.

Maybe that is why it was such a relief to be driven around the island of Aruba by Michael, a bus driver employed by the "Friendly Tours" company. Michael tells his bus passengers about the average annual rainfall on the island (17 inches) and Aruba's sole export (aloe vera). But in between he keeps up a steady patter of kvetching and complaining. The government's either ineffective or corrupt, the high cost of living makes it difficult for the average guy to make ends meet. Life is hard and times are tough. He seems especially interested in the cruel certainties of death and taxes.

"The one way to be rich on Aruba is to be a politician," he says as the bus passes a local governmental office.

We pull into the parking lot of the Santa Anna Church. The main attraction is the oak altar inside the church, carved by a one-armed Dutch artisan. Michael's interest is in the cemetery next to the church, where people are interred above ground in double- and triple-decker tombs that are painted pink or purple or covered with bright blue tile. Some of the tombs have marble face plates, but others are cement slabs, with the name of the deceased written by hand while the cement was still wet.

The island is running out of space for the dead, he says.

"Cremation has to come to Aruba. The government has to do something."

The tour reveals something else that lets travelers know that they are no longer in America. Driving up Aruba's rugged north coast, Michael complains about how many natural rock bridges have fallen down. Even nature disappoints him. He stops at one of the seven remaining bridges to let his passengers walk across it.

Twenty-five feet high with dangerous rocks and pounding surf below, tourists are free to walk up to the very edge of the bridge to peer over. In America, there'd be fences and guard rails and signs with the word "Danger" all over the place.

Back in the bus Michael drives us back to the ship. The closer the bus gets to its destination, the more cheerful he becomes, until finally the passengers seem ready to enter once again their bliss-filled home aboard the Rhapsody of the Seas.

Below Decks
A view from the bridge

Captain Remo rules the ship with quiet intensity

MODERN-DAY CRUISE SHIPS ARE CITIES AT SEA, providing vacationers with a grand adventure. But that adventure comes about because of the hard work of hundreds of crew members who work among the passengers or behind the scenes and live parallel lives "below decks."

One of the most visible of these people is the ship's captain./p

Arnolf Remo spends his days more than 80 feet above sea level on the bridge of the M/S Rhapsody of the Seas. He takes the helm of the fourth-largest cruise ship in the world with a sure hand. During the last week of March he brought more than 2,000 passengers and nearly 800 crew members more than a thousand miles around the southern Caribbean. He makes it look easy.

The captain first appears to the passengers as a disembodied voice over the ship's public-address system.

Captain Remo speaks slowly with an accent redolent of his Norwegian birth and upbringing. The pauses in his speech sometimes sound odd to American ears, "Good morning, ladies and gentlemen. It's a beautiful (pause) day. The sun is shining (pause), and the temperature is 85 degrees Fahrenheit. (Really long pause.) Enjoy your day at sea."

So it turned out to be something of a shock to see the big, handsome man in person. The first thing you think when you see him is, "Wow! A tanned Norwegian! Who would have thought such a creature existed?"

It's Sunday evening. The Rhapsody of the Seas is steaming toward Oranjstad, Aruba, and Captain Remo is hosting a cocktail party (the first of two that night) to meet and greet all the passengers ... all 2,000-plus of them. This big, broad-chested man wears a captain's uniform so white and sharp that it almost hurts to look at him. He stands at the end of a receiving line. He smiles. He shakes the hands of the passengers, and he poses with each one for a picture, taken by the ship's photographers.

(Cruise ships are just nuts about pictures. The photo lab processes between 15,000 and 20,000 pictures a week. They take a picture of you when you leave the ship, when you're cutting a rug on the dance floor, when you stand with the captain, when you sign up for formal portraits behind a backdrop of the ship at night, everywhere but in the shower. These pictures then go on display in the photo shop for you to find and purchase.)

Not a party animal

Captain Remo does this grip-and-grin thing well, but not easily. There is a palpable feel that this is a man who feels most at home on the bridge. At the cocktail party, Remo introduces his staff. He then gives a short speech, the gist of which seems to be "It's A Small World After All." He praises the international make-up of the passengers. He praises the international makeup of the crew. He muses aloud about the world being a better place if everyone learned to live as if they were on a cruise ship.

Remo is a veteran of 100 cruises, and one gets the feeling that this particular part of the job is not what he went to school for.

You don't get to drive one of these megaships by taking a correspondence course offered on the back of a matchbook cover.

Remo first set sail in 1967, working as a seaman on cargo ships around the world. In 1970, he returned to the Norwegian Naval Academy for two years. He earned his master's license in 1976 and began working for Royal Caribbean International the following year. A series of promotions from chief officer to staff captain followed. In 1989, he was selected as superintendent of the French shipyard where the M/S Majesty of the Seas and the M/S Monarch of the Seas were built. In 1991, he served as captain of the Majesty. Presently, he is on the

Rhapsody. Royal Caribbean tends to keep captains and bridge officers together for two or three years a time.

The man knows his boats.

And he has power.

On this floating city, Arnolf Remo is the head honcho, the Big Mackerel, the Great Herring. His word is law for the 3,000-plus passengers and crew. In fact, the only order he can't countermand is the medical recommendation of the ship's doctor. (Just like on "Star Trek," which was why Dr. "Bones" McCoy was always such a pain in the neck to Captain Kirk.)

The captain must combine technical skill with the very real power he wields. Nowhere is this more evident than on the bridge of the ship when it enters or leaves port.

Jennifer Grace, an on-board administrative assistant, invites us up to the bridge on Tuesday evening as the ship pulls out of Curacao. In return, we promise to stay out of the way.

The ship is scheduled to get under way at 6 p.m., but an engine light that isn't supposed to be lit is flashing red. The captain decides we aren't going anywhere until somebody gets the light turned off.

The bridge is the one place on board where you can see the whole ship from the bow to the stern. It's on Deck 8 and looks like some strange combination between the Millennium Falcon from "Star Wars" and the HMS Bounty. Computers and display terminals are everywhere, yet there is a paper map on table where the crew hand-plots its course. Radar sees miles ahead, but Remo will pick up binoculars to peer into the distance. Wrap-around windows (with huge windshield wipers) provide a panoramic view of the sea. Five radar screens silently scan the waters ahead.

"This shows where we'll be in 12 minutes," says First Officer Stern Bjorheim, pointing at a radar screen. "The rules of the sea are a lot like the rules of the road. Not everybody obeys them. Luckily, everything at sea happens slowly."

"This takes something"

Bjorheim looks like a Scandinavian Beach Boy and sounds like he would prefer that things happen a little more quickly. He stands near what is the equivalent of the ship's throttle and talks often about how fast the ship could go at full speed. You get the feeling that, as a teen-ager, he was always pestering his father for the keys to the boat so he could take her to the fjords and "really open her up to see what this baby can do."

He takes obvious pride in the artistry and technology of the Rhapsody of the Seas: "You can build a hotel anywhere," he says, referring to the main part of the ship. "All you need is to choose the curtains and figure out where to put the fountains. But this."

He pauses and looks around the bridge.

"This takes something," he says.

The sun is going down, and the engine light is still lit. Jennifer Grace points out the people responsible for getting us safely out of port: "In the bow, you can see the chief officer, the chief carpenter and five able seamen. In the stern is the ship's bosun and more able seamen."

On the bridge is the captain, the staff captain, the first officer, the safety officer, the environmental officer, the hotel director, the quartermaster and a harbor pilot.

The harbor pilot is the local expert on the particular channel we're sailing through. He comes on board shortly before the ship pulls out of port. When the ship is under way, he leaves the bridge for the Deck 1, where he jumps onto a waiting tugboat. Grace describes his presence, which is legally required, as absolutely essential for safety reasons. For the hour I was on the bridge, the harbor pilot drank coffee, smoked cigarettes and looked out the window. He may have offered the captain a few words of advice, but Remo's been around this particular block more than once.

Since the captain has a little time on his hands, I figure I'll ask him a few questions: "Captain Remo, what to do you have to do to be a captain of a ship this size? How long does it take?"

Remo does not suffer fools gladly. He gives me a strange look.

"Some people are never able to do it," he says simply.

Does he ever have a sense of unreality about his ability to control a ship this large with a joystick? Another strange look from the captain.

"Do you ever feel that way when you drive a car and control all those tons with two fingers on the steering wheel?" he asks. "This is your life. This is what you do." The captain talks about even bigger ships under construction, ones that can hold 3,000 passengers plus a wedding chapel and ice-skating rink.

He says training on those ships takes place in a simulator: "You want to finish your mistakes there, before you go to sea," he says with a smile.

Suddenly, the light problem is fixed and the captain moves into action. Because ships are too large for something like side-view mirrors, the bridge has starboard and port bridge wings ... outside platforms with their own set of controls. The captain begins tonight on the starboard side ... the right side of the ship. You can hear the thrusters and engines roar dully to life 100 feet below us. Remo backs the ship up, turning slightly before heading out to sea. At one point, he abruptly leaves the bridge wing for the more panoramic view in the center control area.

The lights are off in the main bridge, control panels flickering in the darkness. The whole scene on the bridge looks like something out of "Das Boot." It is thrilling and awe-inspiring to watch this small group of men take control of something so large and powerful. There is a quiet intensity in the way they move and stand and speak quietly to another with small, clipped phrases. It's almost beyond human scale. You watch these men pilot this ship, and you begin to believe that nothing is impossible.

Just a regular guy?

Dinner at the captain's table is something of an honor. Remo tries to come across as just a regular guy to the seven of us sharing his table. He talks about his imminent vacation back home in Norway, about how his wife will have a list of household chores waiting for him after 14 weeks at sea. He complains about paperwork and bosses.

But even here, in this casual setting, I can see the power he has. The slightest gesture of his hand, just the raising of an eyebrow brings a waiter running.

There are some people who don't understand exactly how busy the captain is, Grace says. They think that if they have a problem with their room or their pillow's not fluffed properly, they need to complain to the captain.

"Too much "Love Boat'," she explains.

At dinner, Remo lets those at his table in on what he plans to do that evening.

"I'm going to pack for my vacation," he says. Sometimes, as much as he loves being in the captain business, he can't wait to get home for a long vacation.

Because one man's floating paradise is another man's job.

BELOW DECKS
Room at the top: Luxury fit for a king

THERE'S LUXURY. AND THEN THERE'S REAL LUXURY.

The normal staterooms on board the Rhapsody of the Seas are nice and, for lack of a better word, "cozy." The bathrooms in particular are a marvel of the art of space management. Toilet, sink and shower occupy a space no bigger than two 1950s-style phone booths. The size of the bathrooms is a running joke among the passengers, the crew and even the comedians who come on board to entertain.

Spacious accommodations are available on board the ship, however. But they will set you back more than the approximate per-person cost of $1,400-$2,000 the regular staterooms go for. Suites are available on Deck 8, just aft of the bridge area, which affords its tenants some of the best views on board. And one of them, known as the Royal Suite, is the nicest and priciest of them all.

At a cost of $5,349 per person, you get a separate bedroom with a king-size bed and a television that rises out of the top of a console, a private balcony, a whirlpool bathtub (that's right: an actual bathtub on a cruise ship ... a true rarity), a shower that doubles as a sauna and a living room with a queen-sized sofa bed.

But that's not all: A pristine white baby grand piano sits in the living room as well, right next to the refrigerator and wet bar. (If you can't play the piano, don't worry. It's programmed to play itself.) In addition, there is a dining table, entertainment center, private bathroom, vanity area and remote-control curtains.

Oh, and one more thing: a doorbell.

The only question is, if you stay in the Royal Suite, is there any possible reason to leave it during the course of the cruise?

BELOW DECKS
Always at the ready

From hospitals to jails, the floating city has it all

THE M/S RHAPSODY OF THE SEAS, the fourth largest cruise ship in the world, is designed to carry her passengers around the seas in a kind of pampered luxury. She's designed to give her passengers a week's worth of paradise.

But even in Eden, danger can lurk. And trained personnel are prepared to deal with matters of life and death.

If it weren't for the gentle rocking of the ship, it would be hard to tell the on-board medical facility from a clinic in a small Mid-western town.

There are small differences: The waiting room has no magazines in it, no canned music playing. A 4-page document on the wall lists services ranging from Breathalyzer tests to enemas. At the receptionist's window, a small bowl sits on the ledge. But there are no lollipops or breath mints in it. It's filled, rather, with small, brown packets of seasickness pills. Unless the motion sickness is severe, the doctor doesn't even need to see the passenger, who just walks in, picks up a dose or two and leaves.

Dr. Inge Matthiesen-Hopkins, is one of the five medical staff on the ship. Two doctors and three nurses serve a patient base of 3,000 crew and passengers.

"Everything that happens in a city happens here," she says, although she admits that seasickness is not very common on dry land. But the most common complaints at sea are similar to those from the shore-side patients. She treated the same common colds and infections for years as a private practice physician in her native Sweden.

She doesn't see that many sunburn patients any more: "Most people have learned how to use sunblock."

Once in a while, though, one patient out of the 10 to 15 that she or her colleague will see on an average day presents her with an unusual case.

Matthiesen-Hopkins sits at her desk in the Rhapsody of the Seas medical facility. Things are slow now, with no patients in the hospital beds and no appointments to keep. But it was busy earlier in the day:

On Monday, March 29, a male passenger attempts to swallow a vitamin-C pill. It gets stuck going down. Rather than take a drink of water, the man picks up a swizzle stick with a ball on one end and uses it to shove the pill back down his throat. He loses his grip on the swizzle stick, and both the vitamin C and the stick go down the hatch.

"We sent him to the hospital in Aruba," says Matthiesen-Hopkins. "It looked like surgery was indicated, but they were able to hook the swizzle stick with a scope and pull it out. The patient is fine and back aboard the ship."

Matthiesen-Hopkins shows her visitors around the several rooms that make up her "hospital." It's clear that a cruise ship is no place to go for delicate neurosurgery, but the compact clinic seems well-equipped to take care of the most common emergencies. The X-ray machine, the defibrillator heart-starting machines, the prescription drugs, the splints and material for making casts are all within reach in the big room that could double as an operating room.

"I could perform an emergency appendectomy here," she says. "I haven't, but I've heard of doctors on other ships who have."

Bedside manner

An appendectomy on the high seas might be a little unnerving for a passenger (or crew member), but then again, so is any illness experienced far from home, which is why Matthiesen-Hopkins believes that cruise-ship doctors need a special sort of bedside manner.

"People feel confined and very far from home. And on board, you can't really get a second opinion. But then again, sometimes people who need to go to the hospital begin to feel a little better the next day and don't want to go to the hospital. We have to tell them, heart patients especially, that we don't have the staff to monitor them 24 hours a day," she says. They just can't stay in one of the five beds available.

There are times when all the on-board medical technology can't save a patient. Behind a door incongruously marked "OXYGEN," Matthiesen-Hopkins reveals a morgue of sorts: a tall stainless steel refrigerated structure with three berths.

The disposition of the dead on ship can be a complicated affair, she says, depending on the wishes of the family and the immigration laws.

Matthiesen-Hopkins' work on board is not limited to the crew or passengers who find their way to Deck 1. She and her colleagues are responsible for the crew's annual physicals. She also oversees the weekly medical emergency drills. When the words "Alpha! Alpha! Alpha!" sound over the ship's public address system, the doctor, her staff, and 10 trained crew members scramble to a simulated emergency. The 10 crew members are there mostly for crowd control, she says, so that the "patient" can be taken care of.

The doctor recognizes the unusual nature of her practice at sea.

"You have to be a born gypsy to enjoy this life at sea," she says of her regular three months on ship before a vacation.

Matthiesen-Hopkins must be a sort of gypsy. She's worked on Royal Caribbean cruise ships for five years. She thinks carefully when considering what would be a really unusual medical circumstance at sea.

"Delivering a baby would be exciting," she says.

Law and order

"A problem comes, you've got to sort it out."

In a clipped, "understatement-is-all" London accent, Ian McLeod describes his work as security officer on board the M/S Rhapsody of the Seas.

The chief law enforcement officer for this floating city is, like all security officers on Royal Caribbean ships, retired from the British Royal Navy. McLeod served 22 years in the armed forces before joining the company as a safety officer. He has a staff of eight Filipinos (six males, two females) who discreetly enforce the rules on board. A Filipino security staff is standard on Royal Caribbean cruise ships.

The passengers on this cruise are a particularly law-abiding bunch.

"The more expensive the cruise, the older the passengers, the less crime you have. This is a fairly expensive cruise," he explains.

That is not to say that the odd passenger can't act up and act out./p

McLeod talks about an incident last month that makes him smile now, but at the time, it wasn't very funny:

There was a passenger on board who got a little drunk. And then he got a lot drunk. In the quiet bar, a piano playing softly amid the murmur of voices and the tinkling of glasses, one voice begins to be heard over the others. Over time, it becomes louder, more strident, upsetting the other guests.

"We cut him off, told him he couldn't drink anymore. "I just want to tip the bartender,' he said. We tried to reason with him," McLeod says. "He was having a bit of a marital problem and just getting worse."

In a bar on land, a bouncer can throw somebody out on his ear. It's hard to do at sea, though.

"We confined him to his room. He promptly smashed the TV and damaged the cabin. We told him that we would like to interview him, and could he come with us, please. He didn't take it well, but we're pretty good philosophers. We put him in one of the jail cells. He claimed he was claustrophobic."

McLeod pauses a second.

"He blasphemed," McLeod says, absolutely shocked even a month later. After being checked out by the doctor, the passenger was allowed out of the cell, but only under guard in the crew area. Restraint, says McLeod, can be physical or psychological.

He finally passed out in a crew lounge.

"He slept like a monkey for 24 hours," McLeod says. The now-sober passenger was still not happy. He wanted to know why his wife hadn't visited him. McLeod ordered him off the ship at the next port.

"His wife finished the cruise," he says with a smile.

Peaceful and on tape

McLeod can watch 48 video screens in his office, showing views from all over the ship. They are cleverly placed so passengers don't get a sense that they are being watched. The only time passengers become aware that security is an issue is when they return to the ship after a day's outing and have their bags checked by X-ray and walk through a metal detector.

"I'm afraid we have to go through this to make the ship a comfortable and peaceful place," he says.

McLeod says one of his biggest challenges is keeping illegal drugs off the ship.

"In certain ports we have to keep extra vigilant to deter drug people from influencing the crew to become "ponies' and moving drugs," he says.

Screens are set up discreetly so the crew can be searched.

"If someone is stepping out of line, we need to know about it," he says.

He works hard to maintain good relations with his staff and the other crew members. Sometimes, when his staff lapses into their native language in view of the public, he reminds them to speak English, which is the required language for the entire staff.

"Respect has to be built up over time," he says.

It's night. McLeod rises from his chair in the public lounge on Deck 5 and moves away to his office. He needs to keep an eye on things.

BELOW DECKS
She's friendly ... by profession and by nature

LAURIE RIZZO HAS MORE THAN 2,000 NEW FRIENDS EVERY WEEK.

As cruise director on the Rhapsody of the Seas, she's paid to keep them busy and happy.

It's a big job, one that keeps her running from one end of the ship to the other from early morning to very late each night. She is the first voice many passengers hear each morning. She details the day's events on the ship's public-address system, telling passengers about the "Sunrise Stretch Class" at the Shall We Dance Lounge.

She reminds them of the midafternoon art auctions at the Centrum on Deck 4. She encourages them to "boogie down" on Disco Night at the Viking Crown Lounge at midnight. She is sometimes the last staff member people see at night, leading sing-alongs and acting in skits. She gets the men in the audience at a theater to put on bras and cavort in front of other passengers. In between all of that, she has to find ways to keep her staff of 60 motivated and perky.

The week's entertainers are booked through corporate offices in Miami. Rizzo, though, has some say in which acts perform on what nights. She decides if the comedy jugglers appear the day before or the day after the opera singer.

Every day is a long day for Rizzo.

But she's been doing this for 11 years. That's 11 years of tapping into passengers' desires to let loose for one week out of their lives.

"I'm inspired by the guests," she says, "by their sense of fun and adventure." Even when she doesn't much feel like being "on," she knows she has to be. Two weeks ago, she had the flu, but she still managed to keep the passengers' spirits afloat.

"You just keep going," she says.

In fact, the self-contained world created each week by the passengers and the crew becomes for her the "real" world.

"I'm always disappointed when I go home," Rizzo says of her seven weeks away from the ship after 14 weeks on board. "You go home, and somebody cuts you off in traffic. You say "hi' to people in the supermarket, and they look at you like you're crazy."

In contrast, life aboard the Rhapsody of the Seas is great. Everybody is always so friendly ... not surprising when you consider that most people she comes into contact with are in it's-vacation-be-nice mode. And to top it off, she doesn't have to do her own cooking or cleaning.

Still, in some ways, it is good to get home, to visit her parents and her dog. It's a compressed kind of "quality time" with family and friends.

Once in a while, Rizzo says, she'll take her family or friends on a cruise. It's a sort of "busman's holiday" for her, a chance to see what other cruise directors are up to and develop new ideas for her own work.

She admits she doesn't do much sightseeing while at work or at play, and her lack of a deep, dark tan bears this out.

Rizzo started her career in show business, as a dancer and choreography.

"I still like to dance," she says. She does have one other hobby: It's as quiet and sedentary as the rest of her life is loud and a whirlwind of activity.

"I have a stamp collection," she says.

BELOW DECKS
Facing death, ridicule under the waves

MAYBE WE SHOULD HAVE READ the "Shore Excursions" brochure more carefully.

From the comfort of our peaceful, safe staterooms, Sue and I signed up for "The St. Martin Snorkeling Adventure." I assumed we'd all wind up on a beach somewhere and wade out into the sea slowly. We'd have our flippers on, our masks and snorkels on. We'd ease into the experience.

But no.

The boat takes the two dozen or so of us out to "Shipwreck Cove" (and isn't that a real confidence booster?) and stops over what looks to me to be the Marianas Trench.

"It's only 20 feet deep," Sue says to me.

I didn't believe her for a minute.

To be fair, we do receive some snorkeling instruction before we're expected to jump off the boat to our certain deaths.

The international sign for "distress in the water," we are told, is waving your hands over your head. That's good, I think. That's what I always do when I'm in the middle of drowning. At least I won't have to try to remember some esoteric hand signal while I'm dying.

The main thing in snorkeling is making sure your mask has a good seal. Or maybe the main thing in snorkeling is to remember to breathe through your mouth tube. All I know is that when I jump in the water, my mask fills up with water like something out of a Looney Tunes cartoon, and I'm drinking quarts of the Caribbean.

I sputter to the surface, flapping my flippers. I'm aware of voices over my head, calling to me from the boat.

"Are you all right, Mr. Riley?" the voices say. "Here's an inner tube."

A big tire comes sailing out by my head.

So now I'm trying to clear my breathing tube, keep the water out of my mask and hold onto a an inner tube. Eight-year-olds are flying past me like electric eels. Susan apparently has forgotten the buddy system and is snorkeling away from me.

I decide that 10 minutes of snorkeling is enough to last me a lifetime. I clamber back on board and decide to hit the rum barrel. On board with me is a woman trying to keep an eye on her husband bobbing in the water.

"He really should have his life jacket on," she says to no one in particular. "He's not that strong a swimmer."

He's fine. Sue's fine. The 8-year-olds are fine. And after a few rum punches, I decide that I'm fine, too.

Sue comes back to the ship having had the time of her life communing with nature, feeding tropical fish out of her hand. It was an extraordinary experience for her.

"Well," I tell her, "I'm glad you had a good time. But remember, the sea can be an angry mistress."

She gives me a strange look.

"How many of those rum punches have you had?" she asks.

I just smile. Some secrets you have to carry all the way to Davy Jones' locker.

BELOW DECKS
Credit the purser's office with grace under fire

LET'S SAY YOU'RE A CRUISE SHIP DEADBEAT. OK, to be more charitable, let's say you're a passenger who has seriously underestimated the amount of money needed to pay for drinks and film and souvenirs and shore excursions. All those little extras get tacked onto your credit-card bill. You max out on your Visa card while at sea. What happens then?

The purser's desk swings into action. Strolls into action, actually, in a low-key, "let's-see-how-we-can-save-face-here" manner. A letter slipped under your cabin door requests your presence at the purser's desk to clear up a minor matter that almost certainly is not your fault.

You travel up to Deck 5. You speak to someone like Soren Poulen, who assures you with a smile that this sort of thing happens all the time. In all likelihood, he assures you, your credit-card company is looking out for you.

Since the Caribbean and the Far East are the two worst places in the world for credit-card fraud, it is probable that your credit-card company won't authorize an expense until you give them a call to let them know that you and your credit card are having the time of your life in sunny climes. In the meantime, any other credit will do.

So sorry to have bothered you, a purser will tell you.

The world of the purser's desk on board the Rhapsody of the Seas is totally alien to most Americans. Here are people bending over backward to save you embarrassment and help you keep your dignity.

Even when the credit card is maxed out, even when there is no other credit card, even when you haven't got the cold, hard cash to cover the day's outlays, the pursers are unfailingly polite and cheerful.

"We try to work something out," says Bob Tavadia, hotel director for the Rhapsody of the Seas. "Often, people travel with friends who will cover for them. Sometimes we'll take a personal check. We'll do what we have to to ensure that a passenger has a good time."

The purser's desk is open 24 hours a day to answer questions, handle problems and exchange messages between passengers or between passengers and staff.

And passengers do have questions. One of the questions Soren Poulen hears a lot is this one: "What time is the Midnight Buffet?"

"We try to be nice," he says. "We always say something: 'Oh, around midnight.'"

BELOW DECKS
Goodbye, Paradise! Hello, real world

IT SEEMS LIKE HUMANS CAN TAKE ONLY SO MUCH FUN before the body begins to rebel.

Life aboard the floating city can take its toll. Passengers on the go from early morning to very early the next morning begin to flag toward the end of the cruise.

You see it in the slight impatience parents show with their children.

You see it in the elevators as passengers rely more and more on the carpets to let them know what day it is. Every night, at a little after midnight, each carpet on each elevator is changed, an imprinted reminder that a new day dawns.

"Is it Friday already?" they ask, laughing at one another.

By Thursday night, the decks, bars and lounges are less populated than they've been all week. People are winding down and packing up.

The crew, on the other hand, is steadfast in its upbeat drumbeat of service and entertainment. It would be understandable, however, if they were filled with some sort of apprehension. Friday night is "Tip and Staff Evaluation Night."

Passengers are expected to tip their cabin attendant, head waiter, waiter, assistant waiter and wine steward. They also are asked to fill out a ratings form for these people.

One waiter told a table full of passengers, "If you can't write 'Excellent' on the form, please leave it blank."

On the night before disembarkation, passengers are asked to leave their luggage outside their staterooms. It will be gone in the morning, spirited away by the crew during the wee hours.

The cruise director gently reminds the passengers that, when they pack all their luggage, they need to leave out clothes for the morning. The purser's desk sometimes gets panic calls from near-naked guests who, quite literally, "haven't got a thing to wear."

Some of them will not see their luggage again until they are at the baggage-claim center at their local airport. Hundreds of suitcases and valises lining hallway after hallway, deck after deck, is indicative of an act of faith that the "real world" beyond the Rhapsody of the Seas still operates with some sort of efficiency.

On the way home, people pass indifferent U.S. Customs officials and surly airport-security people. They eat bad airline food and watch lousy airline movies.

It's a blessing of sorts, a sort of limbo for the weary passengers, who, in a very short time, will return again to the "real world": It's a world that won't wait upon them hand and foot. Breakfast in bed is not an inalienable right. And service with a smile is as distant a dream as the impossibly blue waters of the Caribbean.